Jane Putnam Chauven

The Columbian Cook Book

Containing Reliable Rules for Plain and Fancy Cooking

Jane Putnam Chauven

The Columbian Cook Book
Containing Reliable Rules for Plain and Fancy Cooking

ISBN/EAN: 9783744791816

Printed in Europe, USA, Canada, Australia, Japan

Cover: Foto ©Andreas Hilbeck / pixelio.de

More available books at **www.hansebooks.com**

THE

COLUMBIAN COOK BOOK

.... CONTAINING ....

RELIABLE RULES FOR PLAIN AND FANCY COOKING.

CAREFULLY TESTED AND ARRANGED.

By

MRS. JANE PUTNAM CHAUVEN,

ST. PAUL, MINNESOTA:
J. W. CUNNINGHAM & CO., PRINTERS.
1892.

PREFACE.

THE rules given in this Cook Book have been tested, and if carefully followed, I am confident will give satisfaction. All I need say as an introduction to this little work, is that it was compiled at the earnest solicitation of many friends, who were kind enough to think that after an experience of more than a score of years I might prepare a work that would prove useful to many persons interested in the art of cooking, especially to young housekeepers.

JANE PUTNAM CHAUVEN.

A copy of this book will be sent, postage paid, to any address on receipt of 50 cents Address

Mrs. Jane Putnam Chauven,

898 Iglehart Street,

St. Paul, Minn.

BREAD, ROLLS, RUSKS AND BISCUITS.

Good Bread.

The first requisite for good bread is, good flour, second good yeast; the third, endurance. Fleischmann's compressed yeast is perfectly reliable. Bread should be mixed up warm; be careful not to scald the yeast; good kneading is very necessary. The heat of the oven should be moderate when the bread is put to bake; an ordinary sized loaf of bread with the oven at proper temperature will bake in an hour, some test the oven heat by putting in a little flour, if it browns in five minutes it is ready for bread. There are several methods of testing bread to know when it is done; a loaf of bread when done will not burn the hand, if it does the bread should be replaced in the oven. After baking, bread should be taken from the oven and placed where it will be exposed to the air.

Bread.—No. 1.

Pour gradually one quart boiling water on one pint flour, stir to keep smooth, when cool, add one cake Fleischmann's compressed yeast dissolved in one-half cup water, let stand until very light, then add flour to make a stiff sponge, with one teaspoon salt; as soon as sponge rises it is ready for kneading, and after being worked until it does not stick to the hands it is of proper consistency.

2

and may be divided into loaves, put in pans to rise for baking.

Bread to be made up in day time.

Bread.—No. 2.

Put three pints hot water into bread bowl with large tablespoon lard, two teaspoons salt, when cool stir in sufficient flour to make stiff batter, beat smoothly, then add one cake of Fleischmann's compressed yeast dissolved in one-half cup warm water, set to rise, when light work in enough flour to form a dough, then turn out upon a floured bread board and knead twenty minutes to one-half hour, return to the greased bread bowl and let rise till very light, then knead again, divide in loaves, and put in pans to rise for baking, when risen to top of pans, bake from forty-five to sixty minutes.

Bread.—No. 3.

Dissolve one teaspoon salt, one tablespoon of lard or butter, mixed in one quart hot water, when cool add one cake Fleischmann's compressed yeast dissolved in one cup warm water, sift three and one-half quarts flour in a pan (you may not need it quite all) then stir some of the flour into the water until a stiff batter and beat until smooth, now take the spoon out and with the hands work in sufficient flour to form a dough, turn out upon a floured bread board and knead twenty minutes, one-half hour is better as it will make the bread closer grained, return to the greased bread bowl to rise over night; in the morning knead one-half hour, divide into loaves, put in pans to rise for baking; when sufficiently light bake from forty-five to sixty minutes, according to size of loaves.

My Bread, J. P. C.

In following this rule you can use milk or half milk and water, all are good.

Bread.—No. 4.

Early in the morning take one cake Fleischmann's compressed yeast dissolved in one pint warm water, stir in flour sufficient to make stiff batter, cover and set near a fire to rise, when light take another pint of warm water and teaspoon salt, pour this on the sponge, and sift into the bowl six cups flour or as much as will be required to make a dough that may be worked with the hand, knead the dough twenty minutes, divide in loaves, put in pans to rise for baking, cover to keep warm, when risen sufficiently, bake.

Potato Bread.—No. 1.

Boil one pint sliced potatoes, in three pints water, mash, pour over the potatoes the water in which they were boiled, stir in one large tablespoon lard, four tablespoons flour, two teaspoons salt, when cool enough add one cake Fleischmann's compressed yeast dissolved in one-half cup water then work in flour enough to make a stiff dough, turn out upon a floured bread board and knead one-half hour, let rise over night; in the morning knead one-half hour, divide in loaves, rise and bake.

Potato Bread.—No. 2.

Pare and boil two potatoes, mash fine, mix in one teaspoon salt, one tablespoon butter, two pints warm water, when cool add one cake Fleischmann's yeast dissolved in three tablespoons water and flour enough to make a batter, let rise, when light make up into stiff dough, knead well and let stand until very light, then knead again, divide in loaves, put in pans. When raised enough bake. Make up this bread in day time.

Salt-Rising Bread.

Day before baking, about noon, pour one cup of boiling milk over three-fourths cup corn meal, and beat smoothly; set in a warm place. Next morning, early, take a pitcher and put in one cup flour, a scant half-teaspoon salt, teaspoon sugar, then pour in the corn meal and milk and sufficient warm water to make a batter, beat smoothly and leave the spoon in the pitcher; cover with folded cloth; set pitcher in deep vessel of warm water, sufficient to come near top of pitcher. Keep water same temperature. When light, sift some flour in bread bowl, work in a little lard, add half teaspoon salt, pour in the sponge with one pint warm water; mix into a dough little harder than for biscuits, knead well and divide into two loaves; put in pans to rise, when light brush a little melted lard over each loaf and bake from fifty to sixty minutes. When this bread is taken from the oven it must not be covered; set the loaves where the air will get around them a little. When cold wrap them in a cloth slightly dampened; put in tin box or stone jar.

Yeast.

Half-pint yellow corn, roasted to a light brown; one pint hops, loose measure; five potatoes, medium size; three tablespoons salt, two-thirds cup sugar. Put the corn, hops and potatoes in a kettle with two quarts water, boil thoroughly and strain through a colander, then add the salt and sugar; when cool add one cake Fleischmann's yeast, dissolved in water.

Good Yeast.

Two large handfuls of loose hops, three quarts water, six medium-sized potatoes, pared, boiled and mashed; half teacup salt, two tablespoons sugar, two tablespoons flour, mixed in little cold water; two cakes Fleischmann's compressed yeast, dissolved in a little warm water.

Graham Bread.—No. 1.

Take two quarts white flour, dissolve two cakes Fleischmann's compressed yeast in two and one-half pints water, one cup brown sugar, one level tablespoon salt. Let rise over night. In the morning work in Graham flour to make stiff dough, let rise then mold in loaves, put in well greased pans to rise for baking.

Graham Bread.—No. 2.

Two quarts Graham flour, one-half cup molasses, two teaspoons vinegar, one teaspoon soda dissolved in water, and wet the whole with cold water, just enough for a stiff batter. Bake one hour in moderate oven and you will have a delicious loaf of bread.

Our Grand Ma's Breakfast Rolls.

Take three cups of warm milk, three-fourths cup lard and butter mixed, one cake Fleischmann's compressed yeast dissolved in half cup warm water, teaspoon salt, one egg beaten, mix with flour enough to make a stiff dough, let this rise over night; in the morning roll out in a sheet the same as for biscuits, cut with with cake cutter, prick with fork, put on pans slightly greased, and bake twenty or twenty-five minutes.

Tea Rolls.—No. 1.

In morning beat two eggs, have almost boiling one pint new milk, pour it on the eggs and mix well, add one tablespoon butter and one of lard, when cool stir in one cake Fleischmann's compressed yeast dissolved in half cup warm water, work in flour to make stiff dough, which may take two quarts. Let rise till afternoon then make into rolls, put in greased pans, giving time to rise, and bake in time for tea. These are delicious.

Tea Rolls.—No. 2.

Put one pint milk to boil with two tablespoons butter. As soon as milk commences to boil stir in flour as though making mush, beating all the time to keep smooth; when a thick batter remove from fire, stir in one pint cold milk, let cool, then add one cake Fleischmann's compressed yeast, dissolved in a little warm water, one teaspoon salt; work in flour to form a dough; knead on floured bread board until it ceases to stick to the hand. Let raise till afternoon, then roll out half-inch thick, lift from the board and let shrink all that it will, cut with a round or oval cutter, put a bit of softened butter on one edge and fold over, letting the edges come together. Put them close together in the pan, cover well with several thicknesses of cloth, and let them rise more than double their bulk, then bake in oven hot enough to brown instantly, and thus check any further rising in the oven. As soon as they come from the oven, put a teaspoon butter in a cloth, twist the edges together and rub the cloth over the hot rolls; the butter will melt through the cloth and give a gloss to the rolls.

Tea Rolls.—No. 3.

Boil one pint new milk with a piece of butter the size of an egg; then stir, *while hot*, in flour to make a batter, and when about milk warm put in one cake of Fleischmann's yeast dissolved in half cup water; let rise, and when light mix in sufficient flour to make a soft dough. Let stand till very light, then roll out in a sheet half-inch thick, cut in narrow strips, let rise and bake. These are very light and nice.

Rusks.—No. 1.

Dissolve two cakes Fleischmann's compressed yeast in three cups of milk that has been scalded and cooled; two tablespoons butter, and one of lard, one teaspoon salt, one and three-fourth cups sugar, two eggs; mix with sufficient flour to make dough, not too stiff; set in warm place to rise over night. In the morning knead, and make out in rusk, put in greased pans to rise, when light bake from twenty-five to thirty-five minutes.

Louise's Rusk.—No. 2.

One large coffee-cup warm milk, half cup lard, one teaspoon salt, three well-beaten eggs, one small cup sugar, two cakes Fleischmann's compressed yeast, dissolved in two or three tablespoons water. Use flour enough to make smooth dough; stand until very light, then knead it in the form of biscuits, put them in greased tins and let them rise; prick the top of each one when light enough; bake in moderate oven.

Sweet Bread.

One quart new milk, half cup butter, one tablespoon lard, teaspoon salt, two cups sugar, one nutmeg. Dissolve two cakes Fleischmann's compressed yeast in half cup warm water; mix with flour to make dough as for bread; rise over night. In the morning knead a few minutes, then make out in any shape desired, round or long loaves, but have them small; when light, bake.

Beaten Biscuit.

One quart flour, one teaspoon salt, one tablespoon each of butter and lard, one egg; mix with sweet milk; beat for half hour; cut out, prick with fork and bake in hot ven.

Milk Biscuit.

One quart flour, one tablespoon lard, one teaspoon salt, enough new milk to make a stiff dough; work well; beat with a rolling pin half hour; make in biscuit and bake quickly.

Cold Water Biscuit.

Three pints flour, two tablespoons butter, teaspoon salt, mix with cold water; beat half an hour; roll out, prick with fork and bake in hot oven.

Aunt Harriet's Cream Biscuit.

One quart flour, two heaping teaspoons Snow Flake baking powder, two tablespoons butter, one pint thick sweet cream, half teaspoon salt. The dough should be very soft; roll thin, prick with a fork and bake quickly.

Eddies Biscuit.

One quart flour, two heaping teaspoons Snow Flake baking powder, two tablespoons butter and one of lard, half teaspoon salt, enough water to make a soft dough, roll thin and bake quickly for about ten minutes.

Biscuit.

One quart flour, two heaping teaspoons Snow Flake baking powder, one tablespoon butter, one of lard, half teaspoon salt, one pint water or sweet milk, handle as little as possible, roll thin, prick with a fork, and bake quickly. If wished plainer, use one tablespoon shortening.

Whipped Biscuit.

Two eggs, half pint milk, one and half cups flour, half teaspoon salt, one tablespoon soft butter, one teaspoon Snow Flake baking powder. Beat the eggs until light and add them to the milk, put butter, salt and baking powder into the flour and with an egg beater whip the whole until well mixed, then add milk and eggs, still mixing with the egg beater. Turn into gem pans and bake in quick oven twenty minutes.

Spoon Biscuit.

One quart sour milk or butter milk, one teaspoon soda, a little salt, two tablespoons butter or sweet melted lard, and flour enough for a stiff batter, drop in a hot gem pan and bake in a quick oven.

Wafers.—No. 1.

Four cups flour, two tablespoons butter, half teaspoon salt, mix with sweet milk into stiff dough, roll out as thin as writing paper. Sprinkle flour over the baking pan, lay them in carefully and bake quickly.

Wafers.—No. 2.

Rub a teaspoon of butter into a pint of sifted flour, add two pinches salt, and with the white of an egg and a little warm milk mix into a smooth paste. Beat half hour with rolling pin, form into little round balls (size of a pigeon's egg) and roll to the size of a saucer, sprinkle on the pans a little flour, and bake with care. These may be made of oatmeal.

STRAWBERRY SHORT CAKE.

Strawberry Short Cake.

Make a crust with one tablespoon lard and two of butter; mix as for biscuits; roll in two sheets, spread the under one with butter, place the other on top, and bake. When baked separate layers and place mashed, and sweetened, fruit between and on top; or the crust can be baked in one piece and split and buttered after baking. Peach, orange and rhubarb shortcakes are very nice. Serve with cream.

Sweet Short Cake.

Beat a lump of butter, size of an egg, to a cream, add one cup sugar, two eggs, whites and yolks beaten separately; one cup sweet milk, and flour enough to make as stiff as cake. Bake in two jelly tins and spread mashed sweetened strawberries between layers, and on top whole berries with sugar sprinkled over them. Serve with mashed berries sweetened.

PUFFS, MUFFINS AND WAFFLES.

Graham Puffs.

Beat one egg, then add one pint milk, one pint Graham flour, and a pinch of salt, one teaspoon Snow Flake baking powder, one tablespoon sugar. Drop in hot greased gem pans, and bake in hot oven.

Graham Muffins.

Three cups sour milk, half cup molasses, three small teaspoons soda, little salt; mix in one quart Graham flour, and bake in muffin rings.

Corn Muffins.

One cup corn meal, half cup flour, one tablespoon sugar, one and a half teaspoons Snow Flake baking powder, one beaten egg, one and a half cups sweet milk, a little salt. Bake in muffin rings.

Wheat Muffins.

Three eggs, whites and yolks beaten separately; one pint sweet milk, one tablespoon melted butter, two teaspoons Snow Flake baking powder, flour enough to stiffen.

Raised Muffins.

Mix one pint milk that has been scalded and cooled, half teaspoon salt, one cake Fleischmann's compressed yeast, dissolved in a little water, flour enough to make stiff batter. Raise over night; in the morning pour in muffin rings, half full and bake.

Buttermilk Muffins.

Beat two eggs very light, mix with them one pint buttermilk, one tablespoon each of melted butter and lard, one teaspoon salt, same of soda, one quart flour; beat well together. Have the muffin moulds heated, grease well, fill the moulds half full and bake.

Crumpets.

Melt one small tablespoon lard, add to it one egg, one and a half cups milk; beat well; add half teaspoon salt, one teaspoon sugar, one and a half teaspoons Snow Flake baking powder, sifted with two and a half cups of flour. Bake in muffin rings in hot oven, at once, for fifteen or twenty minutes. This makes six crumpets.

Spanish Buns.

One pint milk, two eggs, two tablespoons butter, two of sugar, half teaspoon salt, two and half teaspoons Snow Flake baking powder; stir in flour until it just drops from the spoon. Beat until smooth. Bake in gem pans or patty pans. J. P. C.

Waffles. (Very fine.)

One quart milk, two teaspoons Snow Flake baking powder mixed in flour, enough to make rather a thin batter; one cup melted butter, six eggs beaten separately and whites added last; salt. Bake at once.

Waffles.

One quart sour milk, four tablespoons melted butter four eggs, two teaspoons soda well dissolved in the milk; one quart flour, a little salt. -Beat well and bake.

Breakfast Waffles.

Take three pints of milk, one tablespoon butter, put together in a pan on the stove until the butter melts, add four well-beaten eggs, one teaspoon salt, one cake of Fleischmann's compressed yeast dissolved in two tablespoons warm water, and three pints flour. Let rise over night. In the morning, stir in one level teaspoon soda dissolved in a little warm water. If waffle batter is too thick, thin a little. If liked, grate in little nutmeg, don't use sugar, it has a tendency to make waffle batter heavy.

BATTER CAKES, FRITTERS, CORN MEAL AND MUSH.

Buckwheat Cakes.

Make a smooth thin batter of buckwheat and warm water. For a quart of water allow teaspoon salt, half cake Fleischmann's compressed yeast dissolved in the water. Let rise over night; in the morning add quarter teaspoon soda dissolved in little water. If batter is too thick, thin with little warm water. Bake on a greased griddle.

Indian Griddle Cakes.

Scald one pint of Indian meal, do not make it too wet, add one coffee cup sour milk, teaspoon salt, buttermilk is better if you have it. Stir in the milk one teaspoon soda, add small cup flour and beat well. If the batter should be too thick add more sour milk. Bake well on a hot griddle.

Mother's Batter Cakes.

One quart milk, four cups flour, two teaspoons Snow Flake baking powder, one teaspoon salt; add the yolks of four beaten eggs and one tablespoon melted butter; beat to a smooth batter then add the whipped white of four eggs and stir gently. Bake on a greased griddle.

Sister Kate's Flannel Cakes.

One quart milk scalded with one tablespoon butter. When cool, pour the milk over two or three beaten eggs, and add one quart flour; beat to a smooth batter and add, if convenient, two tablespoons mashed potatoes, one teaspoon salt, stir in one cake of Fleischmann's compressed yeast dissolved in little water. Set to rise over night; in morning, just before baking, put in small teaspoon soda dissolved in a tablespoon warm water. If the batter needs thinning add little milk.

Crumb Cakes.

Put some bread crumbs to soak in a quart of sour milk, rub through a sieve and add four well beaten eggs, two teaspoons soda, one tablespoon melted butter and enough corn meal to make thick. Add Salt.

Pan Cakes.

One pint flour, six eggs, one teaspoon each of Snow

Flake baking powder and salt; make thin batter with two cups milk. Rub a little butter over the bottom of a hot frying pan, pour in a ladleful of batter and bake quickly, Keep warm and serve with maple syrup.

Rice Cakes. ·

One cup of rice boiled in one quart sweet milk, one pint flour, a teaspoon salt, three eggs. Beat well and bake on greased griddle.

Fritters.—No. 1.

Beat two eggs very light with one cup milk, one teaspoon salt, and two cups flour. Beat hard and drop a spoonful at a time in boiling lard sufficient to cover them. Serve with maple syrup.

Fritters.—No. 2.

One and half pints of flour, one pint sweet milk, six eggs, teaspoon salt, one pint milk, or cream if you have it. Drop in hot lard. Fruit, vegetables or oysters may be added to this batter.

Fritters.—No. 3.

One pint sweet milk, two eggs beaten very light, salt spoon salt, four cups flour. with one and half teaspoons Snow Flake baking powder. Drop in hot lard. Batter for fritters is best made up several hours before using.

Corn Bread.—No. 1.

One cup flour, three cups corn meal, three eggs, one and half cup butter, two teaspoons Snow Flake baking powder; one pint milk and little salt.

For Annie.

Corn Bread.—No. 2.

Two cups meal, one cup flour, half cup lard, two tea-spoons Snow Flake baking powder, two eggs, one cup milk, one of water, a little salt. Bake in quick oven.

Virginia Corn Bread.

Dissolve one and half teaspoons butter in one and three-fourths pints boiling milk; into this scald one pint corn meal, when cool add half cup wheat flour, a little sugar, half teaspoon salt and one beaten egg. Mix well together and bake in tins well greased.

Johnny Cake.

One tablespoon butter, one cup corn meal, one cup flour, one egg, one cup sour milk, one level teaspoon soda.

Barley Mush.

To one quart boiling water and a pint of milk add six table spoons of barley meal. Boil one hour slowly.

Corn Meal Mush.

One quart boiling water, one tea cup sifted corn meal, sift in gradually or mix with cold water and pour in the boiling water; salt, and boil half hour, stiring to keep from burning.

Oat Meal Mush.

Boil a pint of water, add teaspoon salt; stir in oat meal until thick, boil slowly half hour. Serve with cream and sugar or butter.

SOUPS.

Soup Stock.

Take five pounds of lean beef, wash and put in cold water without salt, let come to a boil, skim. Add little salt and very little cold water. Let boil six or eight hours, add little pepper, strain and let cool and remove the grease. This stock will keep some time. To prepare soup from this, cut off a slice of the jelly, add water, seasoning or whatever is desired; boil and skim.

Tomato Soup.

Six average tomatoes, peeled and sliced fine in one quart boiling water, when this boils add half teaspoon soda, when this stops foaming add one pint milk, rolled cracker, butter, salt and pepper.

Potato Soup.

Two quarts boiling water, one tablespoon of rice, two good sized potatoes and half onion sliced thin, two teaspoons butter, salt and pepper to taste. Boil twenty minutes.

Amber Soup.

Stock.—Take one knuckle of veal, one small carrot, one small onion, one small turnip. Simmer the day before wanted slowly for nine hours, strain, and let stand over night.

For the Soup.—Remove every particle of fat. Have a cup of tapioca in soak for an hour; take two quarts stock and cook slowly with the tapioca an hour, salt to taste, just before serving add half cup cream.

Beef Soup.

Take a shank of beef with plenty of meat on it and boil five or six hours the day before using. The next day skim off the grease, put the jelly in the soup kettle and one hour before serving add turnips, carrots, onions and cabbage chopped fine, in quantity desired. A little celery improves it. Season with pepper and salt; add a few drop dumplings and three tablespoons rice.

Noodle Soup.

Two quarts soup stock, one large tomato, half of an onion, half bunch celery. Cook all together slowly one and half hours and strain; then add noodles about twelve minutes before serving.

Noodles for Soup.

Three eggs beaten, two tablespoons of water, pinch of salt. Add flour to make a stiff dough, roll thin, sprinkle over flour, roll into tight roll, cut into thin slices and let dry an hour before putting into soup. .

Dumplings for Soup.

One pint of flour, one teaspoon Snow Flake baking powder, one egg, small piece of butter, salt, milk enough to mix stiff. Drop from a spoon and boil twenty minutes.

3

Force Meat for Soups.

Rub the yolks of four hard boiled eggs smooth in a bowl, moistening to a paste with a few spoons of the soup. Mix with these a handful of bread crumbs and the chopped meat, and make into small balls.

Browning for Soups.

A good half cup white sugar, a piece of butter the size of a hickory nut one pint boiling water; heat a sauce pan, put in the sugar and butter and let it brown, taking care that it does not burn, then pour in one pint boiling water. Bottle for use.

Beef Tea.

Take one pound of lean beef chopped fine, (at market) pour over it one pint of cold water let it stand an hour. Then set it on back of the range and let simmer slowly three-quarters of an hour. Strain and salt when used.

FISH.

Fish should be properly cleaned on a dry table and using as little cold water as possible, wipe dry and rub well with salt, place on ice until needed.

To boil fish put in boiling salted water, with a table-spoon vinegar, and simmer slowly, over half hour. Salmon will take about an hour. In frying be careful to have the fish completely covered with boiling hot lard, or part lard and beef fat. In baking fish put in a pan on a rack and put little water in bottom of the pan; if this is not convenient put in baking pan with plenty lard and beef fat, or all lard, water is apt to make the fish break in taking out. If you use water add little vinegar.

Baked Fish.—No. 1.

Make a dressing of bread crumbs, butter, salt and pepper; mix with one egg. Fill the fish, sew up, lay in baking pan with plenty of lard or beef drippings, do not use any water, baste with little melted butter. Bake from fifty to sixty minutes; serve with celery sauce.

Baked Fish.—No. 2.

Fill fish with a stuffing made of one pint bread crumbs, two tablespoons melted butter, one raw egg, pepper, salt and two teaspoons celery seed. Fill the pan half full of water, put the fish on sticks laid cross-wise so that it may not be in the water, cover with an inverted pan and bake one and half hours. Sauce: One tablespoon butter beaten smoothly with one tablespoon flour and one cup boiling water, stir constantly until it boils, then add salt, pepper and one chopped hard boiled egg; pour over the fish when done and serve.

Boiled Salmon.

Sew up in a cloth cover with warm water and salt, let simmer until done which will be about twenty minutes for every pound. Take from the cloth, have ready a hot dish and lay the fish on it, remove as much of the skin as you can, garnish with slices of lemon, and serve with drawn butter, or some other nice fish sauce.

Fried Fish.—No. 1.

When cleaned and dried, dip in Indian meal or flour. Fry slowly in lard or beef fat, sufficient to cover the fish, add pepper and more salt if needed. When brown turn over and brown. When done serve.

Fried Fish.—No. 2.

Cut in pieces; beat up the yolks of several eggs, dip in the fish, roll in grated cracker, have ready boiling lard, drop fish in boiling lard and fry.

Fried Fish.—No. 3.

Have the lard boiling hot, and enough to cover the fish. Cut the fish up in small pieces, dredge with corn meal or flour; fry on both sides until brown.

Fried Mackerel.

Soak and wipe dry, sprinkle with cracker dust or corn meal. Fry brown in hot lard; serve with melted butter and chopped parsley.

Stewed Fish.

Put any kind of fresh or canned fish to boil. Stew one onion, three-fourths tea cup butter, one tablespoon vinegar together. Mix the yolks of four hard boiled eggs, the juice of two lemons, one tablespoon cracker dust, and boil. When done put in salt and pepper. Pour over the fish.

Creamed Fish.

Boil any fresh or canned fish; pick to pieces; mix in one quart milk or half cream, two tablespoons flour, one onion, one cup butter, salt to taste. Set on the fire and stir until thick, then put a layer of the mixture in a deep pan over it, spread crackers and butter. Do this until the dish is full. Bake brown, half hour.

Cod Fish Balls.

One pint minced cold codfish, two mashed potatoes, the yolks of three eggs, season with pepper and salt. Form in cakes and fry in lard.

To Pickle Trout for Tea.

Cut the fish in pieces, put in an earthern baking pan, season with salt, a few cloves, and little cayenne pepper, pour on a cup of vinegar and bake three-quarters of an hour. Pour the liquor over the fish and eat cold.

OYSTERS.

Oyster Soup.

One quart oysters, two pints milk, one pint water and the strained liquor from the oysters; one tablespoon cracker dust, or flour made to a smooth paste with little milk; a piece of butter the size of an egg, salt and pepper to taste, a few pieces of chopped celery if liked. Mix milk, water, the liquor and butter together in a porcelain kettle, then add one tablespoon cracker dust or flour mixed to a smooth paste with little milk. Soon as it reaches the boiling point, throw in the oysters, then add salt and pepper and remove from fire immediately, and turn into a warm soup tureen. By no means let the oysters boil, or they will shrivel. Do not put oysters in until you are ready to serve the soup.

Oyster Pie.

Put rich paste in a deep pan. Put in the oysters, season with butter, pepper and salt, add crushed crackers, and pour in the oyster liquor. When full cover the pan with paste and bake brown.

Scalloped Oysters.

Take one quart oysters and their liquor, put on the stove, in a sauce pan, until they are scalding hot (do not boil one instant.) Have ready a buttered baking dish with two cups bread crumbs in it; on this put all the oysters and liquor, two tablespoons butter, salt and pepper to taste, cover with one and half cups of crumbs, three-fourths cup butter, little more salt and pepper on top of all. Bake until brown.

Scalloped Oysters with Rice.

Put three cups rice to soak over night in tepid water. Next day add three-fourths pint of oyster juice or broth, a few celery leaves and water enough to cover, boil until tender; while warm mix half cup butter; when cool beat an egg and add one cup milk to the egg, stir into the rice adding salt and pepper to taste with a dash of cayenne.

Drain the oysters and add to the rice with all the juice or broth from the quart which may drip through, if any (the oysters may be chopped if liked.) Cover the top of the pan with half cup butter, broken in small pieces and little sweet milk. Bake from thirty-five to forty-five minutes.

Fried Oysters.

Select the largest, put them in a colander to drain, then in beaten eggs and then in cracker crumbs; fry in equal parts of butter and lard until they are brown. They are very good dipped in corn meal instead of crumbs.

Lobster Croquettes.

Two cups finely chopped lobster, half teaspoon salt, one of mustard, a trifle cayenne; mix with one cup cream sauce. Make into croquettes, roll in beaten egg and cracker crumbs and fry in hot lard.

MEATS.

BEEF.

Rule for Boiling.—Fresh meat should be placed in a kettle of boiling water and kept where it will boil slowly, but constantly until done. Salt meat should always be put in cold water, so it may freshen in cooking. Allow twenty minutes to the pound for fresh, and thirty-five for salt meats.

Rule for Roasting.—Keep the meat at a moderate distance from the fire. See that it is kept continually turned and well basted, as much depends upon attention to this.

Rule for Baking.—Place in a pan on a tripod or blocks of wood to keep out of the fat, and put in a hot oven. Allow fifteen minutes to the pound for beef, mutton and veal, and twenty minutes to the pound for pork and lamb. When done the roast should be a rich brown. Remove from oven, sift evenly over with fine salt and it is ready to serve.

Rule for Broiling.—The best way to cook a steak is to broil it over moderately hot coals, turning often and basting with butter. Another convenient way: Have a frying pan hot, grease the bottom but have no surplus fat, put in the steak and as soon as it browns, turn it, keep turning it every minute or two, till the outside is cooked this will keep in the juices. Then cover it and let it cook about three minutes, turn it and let it cook for three minutes more. If it is not a very thick steak it will be done sufficiently by this time. If it is turned often at first it cannot be distinguished from a broiled steak. When taken from the fire baste with butter and season with salt and pepper.

Rule for Frying Steak.—Frying is properly cooking in lard or butter sufficient to cover the meat, and should be boiling hot. The secret of success is frying in haste.

Another way is, to use just enough butter, lard or drippings, sufficient to cook the steak.

Pot Roast of Beef.

Take a stone pot, must be shallow enough to stand in oven, rinse the meat, gash a little with a knife, put it into the pot, if closely crowded all the better, sprinkle well with salt and pepper, cover with a lid, and put a brick on the plate to hold it down. Put no water in the pot, and allow no escape of steam while roasting. Bake in moderate oven four or five hours, according to size of roast.

Roast Beef.

The best pieces for roasting are the first and second cut of the sirloin. The next to be preferred are the first cut of the rib and the back of the rump. Dredge with flour, salt and pepper, place in dripping pan with little water, baste often. If a large piece of beef of ten or twelve pounds, allow fifteen minutes to every pound; a small piece ten minutes to every pound. Make a gravy of the dripping, after carefully skimming off all the grease pour the remainder into a saucepan, mix a little brown flour carefully, so as not to have any lumps, and stir into the liquid while hot, boil three minutes and it is ready to serve.

Potted Beef.

Boil a shank of beef till tender in salt water, slip out the bone and leave to cool, chop the meat very fine and boil in the liquor from which it was taken, adding pepper, spice and celery. Pour in a dish, when cool it is ready for use.

Meat Pie.

Line a dish, as for ordinary meat pies, cut up any cold meat, put in a layer of meat, then one of onions and a few sliced potatoes, previously boiled, then a layer of meat, season with salt and pepper, dredge in some flour, put on water enough to make a gravy, then a top crust. Bake an hour.

Beef Loaf.

Take two pounds of lean beef, chop fine, add a small slice of pickled pork, chopped fine, two eggs well beaten, four soda crackers rolled, salt and pepper to taste, and one teaspoon butter. Make into a loaf and bake. .

Dressed Tongue.

Put a corned tongue in water to soak for ten hours, change the water twice, then boil until tender, split it, stick in a few cloves, one onion cut up, a little thyme, add some browned flour. Have the tongue covered with water in which mix the ingredients, add three hard boiled eggs chopped fine and a glass of wine. Send to table garnished with hard boiled eggs,

Fresh Beef Tongue.

Put a tongue in water sufficient to cover it and let simmer six hours, or until tender, then remove the skin. Slice when cold.

Broiled Beef Steak.

Put a choice steak over a hot clear fire on a buttered gridiron, turn when colored, when done lay on a hot dish, season with salt, pepper and butter; cover for a moment then serve.

Fried Beef Steak.—No. 1.

Sprinkle with pepper and salt, then dredge with flour on both sides. Have ready a hot frying pan, with equal parts of butter and lard or beef dripping sufficient, laying in the steak. When done sift powdered crackers over and serve.

Fried Beef Steak.—No. 2.

Pound the steak and fry in plenty of butter and lard, when steak is done take out, and sprinkle with salt and pepper, cover while making the gravy. For the gravy, take one good tablespoon flour and with the back of the spoon mix ingredients until smooth and brown, being careful not to have too hot. Pour in enough warm water (not hot) to make a nice thick gravy, then add half cup sweet milk, salt and pepper, and let boil two or three minutes then pour into gravy bowl and pour little over the steak.

Hamburg Steak.

To each pound of ground beef take one-fourth pound of chopped beef suet, cut some onion very fine, mix in, season with salt and pepper to taste, make in small cakes and fry, with flour sprinkled on both sides, in beef suet and butter or lard.

French Beef Steak.

Cut up steak in small pieces, fry in butter or whatever you wish, add water enough to cover and stew gently

two and half hours, when nearly done season with salt
and pepper, chopped onion and parsley. When done remove from vessel, then take tablespoon of flour mixed
with a little water to a smooth thin paste, then stir into
broth to make gravy, after which, pour over steak and
serve.

Boiled Corned Beef.

Put piece of corned beef in plenty of cold water, cook
fifteen minutes to the pound; when over half done put in
turnips, when both beef and turnips are done, dish up the
beef and lay the sliced turnips around it, If you like
beef fresh, change the water a second time, while boiling.

Corned Beef for Tea.

Boil until soft enough to pull the bones out, place in
an earthern dish and pour over it the water in which it
was boiled. After removing fat, place a plate on it, and
a heavy weight, have sufficient water so that when the
weights are on it will come to the top of the meat. Let
stand until cold, then cut in thin slices and it is ready
for use.

Beefsteak with Onions.

Pound the steak and fry in equal parts of butter and
lard, then add salt and pepper, now dredge flour over it
and add one cup boiling water. Drain the onions, which
have been boiled, cut them up and put into pan, having
taken out the steak, add a lump of butter and little more
flour, stir and when the onions are brown and thoroughly
heated put in the steak.

Hash.

Chop equal quantities of cold boiled beef and potatoes,
add some salt, pepper and a little water and cook in a

frying pan with butter about the size of hickory nut. To one pint each of beef and potatoes add one or two thinly sliced onions, cook slowly from twenty minutes to half hour. If it gets too dry add little more warm water.

Spiced Beef.

Five pounds of shank boiled five hours with celery seed, drain off, then chop the meat very fine, add pepper and salt to taste and put in a cloth on a platter, cover with a cloth and press it.

Liver and Onions.

Slice the liver thin and soak in salt and water, cut up several onions and put in the frying pan with little water, when tender put in a spoon of lard and fry until onions are brown, take them up and set to keep warm. Fry the liver in the pan, adding more lard; pour the onions over and serve.

Grated Ham Sandwiches.

Cut a good sized piece from the thick portion of a ham, that has been boiled, season with spice, mustard and celery seed. Spread on thin bread and butter.

Tongue Sandwiches.

Grate one pound of cold boiled tongue, mix with it a tablespoon mustard, a little pepper, the mashed yolk of a hard boiled egg, two tablespoons butter, one grated nutmeg and the juice of one lemon. Split and butter some nice biscuit, and spread the mixture between.

VEAL.

Roast Veal.—No. 1.

Take a loin of veal, make a stuffing the same as for turkey, fill the fat with the dressing and secure it firmly

on to the loin, rub the veal over with salt, pepper and
butter, put in a pan with little hot water, baste frequently,
letting it cook until thoroughly done and serve with brown
gravy.

Roast Veal.—No. 2.

Take the breast, rub well with pepper, salt and butter,
dredge with flour, and put in a pan with a pint of boiling
water, a slice of fat bacon, minced onion, place in a very
hot oven, baste, and cook done. Thicken the gravy with
mashed potatoes.

Veal Loaf.

Three pounds of raw veal cutlet, chopped fine, two
slices of salt pork chopped, two eggs, three teaspoons of
salt, one of pepper, two slices of bread crumbed fine, half
cup cream or milk. Make into a loaf, dredge with flour
and bake three hours. It is nice to put hard boiled eggs
through the loaf.

Veal Marble.

Boil a beef tongue the day before it is to be used, and
a like number of pounds of lean veal, grind separately in
sausage cutter or chop as fine as possible; season tongue
powdered sweet herbs, a teaspoon mustard and a pinch of
cloves; season veal same, adding salt, pack in alternate
spoonfuls irregularly as possible in bowls or jars well
buttered, press very hard as you go on, smooth top and
cover with melted butter, when cool, close the vessels.
Keep in cool place, turn out whole and cut in slices.

Veal Oysters.

Cut veal into pieces, the size of large oysters, pound
well and dip into beaten egg, then into rolled cracker and
fry in hot lard, as oysters. A most delicious manner of
cooking veal.   Lulu.

Veal Cutlets.

Dip in beaten egg, when you have sprinkled a little pepper and salt over them, then roll in fine bread crumbs and fry in lard. Add water to the gravy and thicken with flour and pour over the meat.

Veal Fricassee.

Take piece of veal from the breast or ribs, cut it in thin pieces about three inches square and put it over the fire in enough water to make plenty of gravy, After it boils, skim. Add a chopped onion, some leaves or stalks of celery, tied in a bunch and let it cook slowly one and half hours or little longer. Just before taking it up, add a tablespoon butter and one of flour, creamed together. After removing the meat add little chopped parsley. Chicken can be cooked in the same way.

Fried Calf's Liver.

Cut in slices and soak in salt water, season with salt, pepper and sweet herbs. Dredge with flour and drop in boiling lard.

Meat Jelly.

A knuckle of veal, one pound of beefsteak from the round, three pints of water cold, boil after skimming, five or six hours, then take out the meat and separate it from the bones and gristle, cut it into small pieces, with knife and fork return it to the liquor, season with salt and pepper adding celery salt if liked; heat once more and pour into a mould.

Veal Salad.

Boil lean veal until tender, chop quite fine, chop two or three hard boiled eggs and mix with it, take cabbage or lettuce chopped fine, mix with salad dressing and garnish.

CHICKEN.

Roast Chicken.

Prepare a full-grown chicken, fill with dressing the same as for turkey; rub a little lard over the chicken, place in dripping pan with little water, salt, and butter or lard. Bake an hour or more, according to size of chicken. Baste two or three times with butter and water, afterward with their own gravy. Stew the giblets in a little water, when you have removed the fowl to a hot dish, pour this into the drippings, boil up once, add the giblets chopped fine, thicken with brown flour, boil again and send to table in a gravy boat.

Fried Chicken.

Cut chicken in pieces, then wipe dry, have in a pan some butter and lard mixed, dust some flour over each piece, season with salt and pepper, then fry slowly, till brown on both sides. Take them up, put a little water and milk in a pan and some butter rolled in flour to thicken gravy and more pepper and salt if needed. Young spring chickens are only suitable for frying.

Baked Chicken.—No. 1.

Cut up the chicken, salt, and dip in flour, have a dripping pan with plenty of boiling lard, into which lay the chicken and put on the bottom of a well heated oven, as soon as brown turn over the other side and brown, moisten a little flour with water, stir in to make gravy. Veal or lamb chops are nice cooked in this way.

Baked Chicken.—No. 2.

Split the chicken, put in dripping pan, put in the stove without water. When half done take out the chicken and with salt, pepper and butter, return to oven to brown.

Roast Turkey.

Have your dressing prepared, fill the skin of the crop and also the inside, sew it up, put it in the oven, and roast moderately three hours. Dressing—Take bread crumbs, put in a small piece of butter, or a little cream, with sage or chopped onion, pepper and salt, one egg, a small quantity of flour, moistened with milk.

Pressed Chicken.

Take two chickens, boil in as little water as possible until they shall drop from the bones, cut it with a knife and fork, then put it back in the kettle, adding plenty of butter, pepper and salt, heat it thoroughly, slice a hard boiled egg, and place it in the bottom of a dish, pour it on hot, place a weight upon it and put away to cool. It will come out in a form.

A nice way to cook Chicken.

Cut the chicken up, put in a pan, and cover it over with water letting it stew as usual and when done make a thickening of cream or milk and flour, adding a piece of butter, pepper and salt. Have baked a couple of short-cakes, made as for pie crust, rolled thin and cut in squares. This is much better than chicken pie and more simple to make. The crust should be laid in a dish, next to the chicken, and gravy poured over all.

Mother's Chicken Salad.

The best meat of two chickens, minced fine, twice as

4

much minced celery, five hard boiled eggs, four large
spoons melted butter rubbed with the yolks, and the
whites minced fine.   Mix thoroughly with this one and a
half teaspoons mustard; salt and pepper to taste, moisten
the whole with one cup cream or chicken broth and a little vinegar—make pretty moist.   In absence of celery use
cabbage.   Veal salad can be made in the same way.

Chicken Pie.

Joint the chicken, put in a kettle, cover with water, and
let boil until tender, then cut them in small pieces, removing the bones.   Line a dish with pastry made of six
cups flour, one teaspoon Snow Flake baking powder, one
cup lard, one of water, half teaspoon salt.   Sprinkle some
flour over the crust, on the bottom of the dish.   Sprinkle
salt, pepper and more flour on the top, also bits of butter.
Pour as much of the chicken liquid as necessary over the
whole, then spread on the remainder of the crust.   Put
bits of butter over the top and bake.

Roast Duck.

Prepare and roast like other poultry.   Put in a quick
oven and roast from thirty-five to forty minutes.   If liked
rare, half an hour.

Prairie Chicken.

Lard the breast and legs, skewer and tie into shape,
sprinkle with salt, rub little butter upon the breast;
dredge with flour.   Cook in quick oven twenty minutes,
if liked rare; thirty, if well done.

Quail.

Split, clean and wash the quail.   Broil on a buttered
gridiron over a lively fire, taking care they do not scorch,
at first; season, put a bit of butter on each and serve hot.

MUTTON.

Roast Mutton.

The leg of mutton with the bone removed and stuffed like poultry is very nice baked. Put the mutton in a pan a little warm, set in the stove and bake slowly, baste with butter, salt and pepper; just before dishing put some chopped horseradish over it, a little ground mustard if liked, and sprinkle with grated crackers. Serve with mint sauce. Bake about three hours.

Lamb Chops.

Take lamb chop pounded, dip in a preparation of eggs, a little parsley and salt, then roll in powdered crackers and fry same as oysters, only keep well covered while cooking, and you will find it good.

Roast Lamb.

The hind quarter is the most desirable. Put in a pan, dredge with flour, pepper, salt and any kind of herbs you may prefer; put in a hot oven, pour in little water and baste with butter, make a rich sauce. Serve with mint sauce and walnut catsup.

Boiled Leg of Lamb.

Rub with salt a leg of lamb or mutton, tie in a linen cloth and boil slowly two or three hours.

PORK.

Roast Pork.—No. 1.

Make deep incisions in the roast. Boil some potatoes, mash them fine, put in butter, pepper, salt and minced onion; with this dressing fill the incisions, put in the stove and bake slowly three hours. Make brown gravy; serve with apple sauce.

Roast Pork.—No. 2.

Take a large roast, cover with grated bread, pepper, salt, butter, onions, sage and thyme. Place in a pan with water, when nearly done, lay all around some nice cooking apples, when done dish your pork with the apples around it; pour the gravy over it. The roast should be kept covered the first two hours as the bread would get too much baked.

To Boil Ham.

Wash and scrape the ham thoroughly; boil it slowly for three or four hours, according to its size; remove it from the water, skin it, put it on the grate of your roasting pan and let it stand in a moderate oven for an hour, then take it out and dust the fat thickly with fine bread crumbs. Return it to the oven until the crumbs are brown.

Fried Ham.

Put a little butter and lard mixed, in frying pan. Slice the ham very thin and fry, take out and pour in one cup water. Make a thickening of a small tablespoon flour and one cup rich milk into a smooth batter, pour into the water and cook until the gravy is thick. Pour over ham, add salt and pepper.

Ham Toast.

Mince fine the lean of boiled ham, beat the yolks of two eggs and with a little cream and a lump of butter, mix with the ham. Put in a skillet and stir until thick, have ready some slices of toast buttered and lay spoonfuls of the ham on them.

Ham Balls.

Take one and half cups of bread crumbs, and mix with two beaten eggs, chop fine, one pint ham bits and mixing altogether; form in balls and fry.

Fried Pork Steak.

Fry in butter, season with salt and pepper; flavor with some powdered sage.

Spareribs Baked.

Put in dripping pan with little water, season with salt and pepper. Bake half hour.

Roast Tenderloins.

Take three pounds fresh tenderloins, have them split. Boil a small measure of white onions, flavor with sage, pepper and salt, chop and tie up in the loins. Serve with a brown gravy.

Pork must be well cooked.

Baked Pig.

Take a six weeks old pig, score in squares and rub all over with lard, make a dressing of two quarts cornmeal rolled and mixed in boiling water, add to it one cup butter, pepper, salt and thyme. Fill the pig with it and sew up, put in a deep pan with hot water, baste frequently until brown and crisp. Serve with baked apples.

Breakfast Sausage.

One pound sausage, one tablespoon pounded crackers, two eggs well beaten, work and make into cakes. Drop each into a plate of pounded crackers; put in hot frying pan with little lard or butter and fry on both sides.

Sausage Rolls.

Plain paste as for pie, roll the sausages in separate pastes. Bake in the oven till brown.

Sausage Seasoning.

Three even teaspoons powdered sage, one and half even teaspoons salt, one even teaspoon pepper to each pound meat.

Scrapple. (Splendid.)

Take two hogs' heads and cook tender, hash fine, add one teacup of liquor they were boiled in, to each head, pepper, salt and sage to taste.   Thicken it with half corn-meal the other half flour, as stiff as you can stir it with a strong spoon.   Pack in a crock until cold then slice and fry a nice brown.

Cold Meat Croquettes.

One pint cold chopped meat, one half pint milk, one tea-spoon salt, a little pepper, one tablespoon butter, two tablespoons flour, a little onion juice.   Mix butter and flour together and add to the boiling milk, stir until it thickens, then add the salt and meat, which must be chop-ped fine.   Set away to cool, and when cool beat one egg to dip the croquettes in after they have been rolled into shape, then roll in crumbs and fry.   Any kind of cold meat can be used in this way; veal is very nice.

Cold Meats.

Take the remains of cold ham, mutton or roast beef, chop fine with hard boiled eggs, two heads of lettuce, a bit of onion; season with pepper, salt and vinegar; serve cold.

Pot Pourri.

Take cold chicken (or any cold meat), chop fine and put in a stew pan with warm water, pepper, salt and min-ced onions, cook half hour, put in baking pan with grated bread crumbs, and teacup cream or milk.   Bake brown.

SAUCE FOR MEAT AND FISH.

Italian Sauce.

Put a lump of butter in a stew pan with some mushrooms, parsley, onions and one laurel leaf, cut fine; set over the fire for some time; shake in a little flour, moisten with a glass of white wine, the same of soup stock, with salt and pepper. Boil half hour. Serve with any meats.

Onion Sauce.

Boil one pint milk, season, add tablespoon butter and one of flonr moistened with cold milk; when thick put in some chopped pieces of onion already cooked.

Drawn Butter.

Half teacup butter, two tablespoons of flour, rub together and stir into one pint boiling water.

Melted Butter.

Two large tablespoons butter cut into small pieces, put in stew pan with large tablespoon flour and a cup of new milk; shake over the fire until it begins to simmer, then let boil. It should be as thick as cream.

Sauce for Fish.—No. 1.

Butter the size of a walnut, put into one pint milk, thicken with flour; let it first simmer then boil, add two hard boiled eggs chopped fine, salt and pepper to taste.

If you wish lobster sauce add quarter can of lobster chopped fine.

Sauce for Fish.—No. 2.

Two hard boiled eggs, two cold boiled potatoes grated, one teaspoon grated onion, one teaspoon made mustard, one of salt, little pepper, four teaspoons salad oil, two teaspoons vinegar; strain through a sieve. This is nice for baked or boiled fish.

Egg Sauce.

Boil four eggs hard, first chop half the whites, then put in the yolks and chop altogether, put in one cup butter, let boil; add juice of one lemon if liked; season with thyme, salt, pepper and chopped parsley.

Maitre d'Hote Sauce.

Add to one cup of fresh made drawn butter, the juice of one small lemon, chopped parsley, minced onions and thyme, cayenne pepper and salt; beat while simmering. Serve with meat or fish.

Game Sauce.

Take veal soup or gravy, squeeze in the juice of several large oranges, a glass of wine, tablespoon currant jelly; let boil. For wild ducks or wild goose.

Celery Sauce.

Chop several large bunches of celery, stew in water until tender, add one tablespoon vinegar, a little salt and pepper, pour in teacup cream and let simmer. To be served with boiled meats or wild fowls.

Mint Sauce.

Three tablespoons of vinegar, two of mint, one of white sugar, one of salt; mix ten minutes before using. To be served with spring lamb.

Salmon Salad.

Take one can of salmon, drain the fish and pick it to
pieces, removing all the bones and pieces of skin. Chop
double the quantity of celery, lettuce or cabbage and mix
with it; use mayonaise dressing and garnish with sliced
lemons.

Caramel Coloring.

Put into a sauce pan (porcelain) one cup sugar and
tablespoon water, stir it constantly over the fire until it
has turned a bright darkish brown color, being very careful not to let it burn or blacken, then add a teacup of
water and little salt; let it boil a few minutes longer, cool
and strain. Put away in a close corked bottle and it is
always ready for coloring soups or gravies.

VEGETABLES.

All green vegetables must be washed thoroughly in cold water and dropped into water which has been salted, and is just beginning to boil. If the water boils a long time before the vegetables are put in, it loses all its gases. The vegetables will not look green nor have a fine flavor.

The time of boiling green vegetables depends very much upon the age, and how long they have been gathered. The younger and more freshly gathered the more quickly they are cooked.

The following is a time table for cooking:

Potatoes boiled...30 minutes.
Potatoes baked..45 minutes.
Sweet Potatoes boiled...45 minutes.
Sweet Potatoes baked..1 hour.
Squash boiled...25 minutes.
Squash baked..45 minutes.
Green Peas boiled..20 to 40 minutes.
Shell Beans boiled..1 hour.
String Beans boiled...1 to 2 hours.
Green Corn...25 minutes to 1 hour.
Asparagus..15 to 20 minutes.
Spinach...1 to 2 hours.
Tomatoes fresh... 1 hour.
Tomatoes canned...30 minutes.
Cabbage...45 minutes to 2 hours.
Cauliflower...1 to 2 hours.
Dandelions...2 to 3 hours.
Beet Greens...1 hour.
Onions...1 to 2 hours.
Beets..1 to 5 hours.
Turnips White...45 minutes to 1 hour.
Turnips Yellow..30 minutes to 2 hours.
Parsnips...1 to 2 hours.
Carrots..1 to 2 hours.

Turn Over Potatoes.

Take two cups mashed potatoes and mould with the hands into a flat round cake, if necessary adding flour to make it moulding consistency. Put in any kind of chopped meat, and a lump of butter the size of a hickory nut, turn over the sides of the cake and pinch the edges as you would a turn over pie. Fry in hot lard, after dipping in egg and bread crumbs. You can use chopped oysters if wished.

Potato Puffs.

Two cups mashed potatoes, one cup milk, two tablespoons melted butter, two eggs well beaten, little nutmeg if liked. Stir in butter first, then eggs, milk and salt; pour in buttered dish and bake in quick oven till brown.

Scalloped Potato.

Pare and slice thin potatoes, let them stand in cold water two hours, sprinkle a buttered dish with cracker crumbs, then a layer of potatoes, some bits of butter, pepper and salt, so on until the dish is filled; having crumbs and butter on top.

Saratoga Potatoes.

Pare and slice very thin potatoes, let them stand one hour in water with a piece of alum the size of a pea, wipe dry and fry in very hot lard, a light brown. Salt while hot.

Potato Balls.

Take one pint mashed potatoes highly seasoned with salt, pepper, celery salt, chopped parsley and butter, and moisten with a little hot milk; beat one egg light, add part of it to the potato, shape into smooth round balls, brush over with the remainder of the egg and bake on a buttered tin till brown. Be careful and not get them too moist. These can also be fried in beef drippings.

Stewed Potatoes.

Pare and slice potatoes, put them in a sauce pan with milk enough to cover them, let them boil till done, thicken with little flour smoothed in cold milk, add a good piece of butter, a little salt and pepper to taste. A little finely chopped parsley may be added.

Baked Potatoes.—No. 1.

Put in a hot oven; when done pierce with a fork to let steam escape.

Baked Potatoes.—No. 2.

Bake and when they are done, cut lengthwise and put between butter, salt and pepper, close together and serve hot.

Baked Potatoes.—No. 3.

Pare and boil ten minutes in salt water, put in a pan and place in the oven. Baste with pork or beef drippings.

Fried Potatoes.—No. 1.

Take cold boiled potatoes, peel and slice thin; fry in butter or drippings until brown; season with salt and pepper.

Fried Potatoes.—No. 2.

Take cold boiled potatoes, slice thin put a piece of butter in skillet and when hot put in potatoes with little hot water, add pepper and salt; when nearly done add a little milk.

Stewed Tomatoes.

Peel and chop tomatoes, season with salt and pepper, minced onion and a little sugar. Put in a sauce pan and stew; add a few broken pieces macaroni and butter.

Raw Tomatoes.

Pare with a sharp knife and slice a plateful of ripe tomatoes; set on ice; pour over a dressing of vinegar, olive oil, pepper and salt with a tablespoon sugar.

Hot Slaw.

Chop cabbage fine, sprinkle over with flour, put a small piece of butter over the fire to melt; salt and pepper the cabbage and put in the pan with the butter. Mix half cup cream, half cup vinegar, one egg, one tablespoon mustard, teaspoon sugar and heat thoroughly. Serve warm.

Cold Slaw

One cup milk or cream, one cup vinegar, one small cup sugar, three eggs beaten very light, a lump of butter the size of an egg, one heaping teaspoon mustard, pepper and salt. Cook until like custard, when cool, pour over cabbage cut very fine. A little chopped celery is an improvement.

To Boil Cabbage.

Wash and cut up a head of cabbage; drain after soaking and put in a pot with a piece of fat bacon, season with red pepper. Boil until done.

Cauliflower.

Remove the outside leaves, cut in pieces, put in boiling water; simmer two hours, Drain and serve with melted butter.

Cabbage Souffle.

Chop cabbage small and boil in salted water until tender, drain off water, pressing with a spoon. To two quarts of boiled cabbage allow four eggs beaten separately, one tea cup butter, one of rich milk, salt and pepper to taste; mix well; bake twenty minutes in buttered baking dish; serve hot. For small family halve this.

Mrs. W. P. A., Mt. Vernon, Ohio.

Stewed Beets.

Wash three large beets, without breaking the skin or cutting off the tops or roots too closely, boil them an hour in a little salt and water, peel and slice them and boil another hour in the following sauce: Mix together in a sauce pan, over the fire, one large tablespoon of butter and also one of flour, the same of vinegar, stir in a pint of boiling water, season with pepper and salt to taste.

Beets.

Wash them, put on to boil without cutting the roots; boil one hour or until tender, then slice and dress with melted butter. Sprinkle with sugar before serving if liked.

Snap Beans.

Boil in salt and water until tender; drain and serve with butter, cream and pepper.

Cymlings.

Peel and boil, run through a colander; season with salt, pepper, cream and butter. Cook very slowly.

Stewed Celery.

Cut in small pieces and stew; when tender add cream, butter and a little flour. Season to taste.

Stewed Mushrooms.

Peel fresh mushrooms, sprinkle with pepper and salt, put in a sauce pan with a little water and a tablespoon of butter, let boil ten minutes, pour in pint of cream or rich milk, thicken with flour.

Asparagus.

Scrape the stems, tie in bunches, throw into boiling water and boil twenty minutes. Have slices of bread toasted and dish the asparagus on it, pour over melted butter. Asparagus may be boiled, stirred in butter and fried.

Scalloped Onions, Cauliflower or Aspargus.

Boil either vegetables until tender, then put in baking dish, and pour over sauce made of one tablespoon of butter rubbed into one and half tablespoons flour, pour over it one pint hot milk and cook until like custard. Bake half hour; cut cauliflower or asparagus into small pieces, before pouring over the sauce.

Egg Plant.

Peel and cut the plant in slices less than half an inch thick; immerse in salt and water over an hour, drain and dip each slice in beaten egg and bread crumbs, and fry brown.

Parsnip Balls.

Boil in salted water till very tender, mash and season with butter, pepper and salt, add a little flour and two well-beaten eggs; form into small balls and fry in hot lard.

Baked Tomatoes.

Take six large ripe tomatoes, skin and cut into small pieces, spread a layer in the bottom of bake dish, season well, put a layer of coarse bread crumbs over the tomatoes, with plenty of butter; continue this until the dish is full, having bread crumbs on top. . Bake one hour. Canned tomatoes can be used, but do not bake so long. Sliced onions cooked in this way are very nice.

Turnips.

Boil and mash; season with cream, butter, pepper and salt. Turnips are nice boiled with fresh pork.

Baked Corn.

Fill a baking dish with corn, cut or scraped from the cob; cover the corn with milk; season with butter, pepper and salt. Bake two hours.

Green Corn Cake.

Six ears of grated corn, the yolks of two eggs, a little salt, three rolled crackers; grease the griddle, drop from the spoon and bake twenty minutes.

Carrots.

Scrape the carrots, slice very thin and boil in salt and water three-quarters of an hour, drain off the water and add one cup milk, a little pepper, butter and salt and two teaspoons cornstarch. Return to stove and cook for five minutes before serving.

Succotash.

Boil one quart lima or string beans until tender, cut down the middle the grains of one dozen ears corn, and scrape. Drain off water from beans, add the corn, season with salt, pepper and a good lump of butter. If too dry, add little cream or milk. Cook twenty minutes after adding the corn.

Minced Spinach.

Wash spinach carefully and boil until tender, drain or rub through a colander or chop fine; then put in frying pan a good lump of butter, the spinach, salt and pepper to taste; when hot put in three tablespoons cream. Garnish with hard boiled eggs.

Baked Beans.

Soak one quart beans over night, pour off the water and cook in fresh water until they crack open, then put into a deep earthen dish, cover with water add one teacup sweet milk, put in the center of dish half pound of parboiled pork, which should be scored across the rind. Bake slowly four hours, keep covered with water until two-thirds done, then allow them to bake brown.

SALADS.

Potato Salad.

Boil potatoes; when cold slice them thin, add an onion chopped fine, season with salt and pepper; moisten with vinegar and sweet oil; twice as much vinegar as oil, added gradually. Place it in a dish lined with lettuce. Keep cool till wanted.

Salad Dressing.

Two tablespoons mustard, one of butter, one teaspoon salt, one tablespoon flour, one of sugar, yolks of two eggs

5

beaten, one and half teacups vinegar, three tablespoons
of cream or milk. Mix mustard, sugar, flour, salt in a
little cold water, pour on eggs vinegar and butter; set
over hot water. Just before taking up add cream and
when taken from heat beat with egg beater.

Mrs. L. H. C.

Mayonaise Dressing.

Yolks two hard boiled eggs and one raw, half teaspoon
salt, a dash of cayenne pepper, half teaspoon dry mustard,
one teaspoon powdered sugar, half cup olive oil, one tablespoon vinegar. Mash the cooked yolks, add raw one and
mix until perfectly smooth, then add the salt, pepper, sugar
and mustard; mix and work again, then the oil a few
drops at a time, stirring all the while; then the vinegar
by degrees. Those who object to olive oil can use instead
one tablespoon melted butter and cream enough to make
half teacupful.

Cabbage Salad.

One quart chopped cabbage, three hard boiled eggs,
cut fine, put in a dish with layers of salt and pepper between. Take one tablespoon butter, two teaspoons of
sugar, one of flour, half teaspoon mustard, one cup of
vinegar and one raw egg, stir all together and let come
to a boil, pour on the cabbage and mix well. Lettuce or
celery chopped is nice prepared in this way.

Tomato Salad.

Peel with a sharp knife and cut six large tomatoes in
slices. Take one tablespoon of oil, one of vinegar, teaspoon of mustard, salt and pepper; mix and pour over the
tomatoes.

Buttered Toast.

Toast bread to a delicate brown, dip in boiling water, containing a little salt; spread with butter and keep hot.

Cream Toast.

Toast slices of bread thin, lay in a covered dish and pour boiling water over; pour the water off and let drain. Put one pint rich sweet milk or cream on the stove in a quart cup, add three tablespoons butter, two beaten eggs and a tablespoon flour or cornstarch, little salt. Let boil up once and pour over the toast.

Ham Toast.

Mince some cold boiled ham very fine, stir in a pint of cream with pepper, mustard, butter and two eggs. Boil and pour over nicely brown toast. Set in oven to dry.

Welsh Rare Bit.

Grate one pint cheese, sprinkle on it half teaspoon mustard, one-fourth teaspoon salt and a sprinkle of cayenne. Heap this on slices of buttered toast; put in the hot oven for a few moments and when the cheese begins to melt, serve at once.

Cheese Fondu.

One cup rolled crackers, one cup milk, three-fourths cup chopped cheese, two eggs, whites and yolks beaten separately. Bake about twenty minutes in a quick oven; serve immediately.

Frank's German Pan Cakes.

Three eggs, half cup cream, a very little flour, a pinch of salt. Put in a greased pan and bake.

Baked Omelet.—No. 1.

Beat six eggs very light without separating yolks from whites, add half cup milk, one tablespoon melted butter, salt to taste, and pepper if desired. Pour into a buttered dish, bake until high and brown; serve instantly.

A plain Omelet.

Melt one tablespoon butter in a hot pan; beat together four eggs, a tablespoon of milk and a scant teaspoon salt, pour this mixture into the hot pan and shake vigorously until the egg begins to thicken. Let the bottom brown then run a knife around the edge, fold the omelet and turn on a hot dish.

Rice.

Pick and wash in warm water, put in a sauce pan, cover with boiling water, boil fifteen minutes and salt; place a lump of butter in the middle and send to the table.

Macaroni with Tomatoes.

Take one quart of beef soup and put twelve sticks of macaroni in it; boil twenty minutes or until the liquor is absorbed; lay in a buttered baking dish, slice one dozen tomatoes and spread over the top, cover with one cup butter, then sprinkle with cracker dust and grated cheese. Bake until tomatoes are done.

Macaroni with Oysters.

Boil one pound macaroni, pour off the water; put in a buttered dish a layer of macaroni and oysters alternately, a ld butter, pepper and salt, then put grated crackers over the top and bits of butter and pour in a cup milk. Bake half hour.

PICKLES.

French Pickles.

One colander of sliced green tomatoes, one quart sliced onions, one colander of pared and sliced cucumbers, two handfuls salt; let all stand twenty-four hours, then drain through a sieve; add half ounce of celery seed, one tablespoon tumeric, one pound brown sugar, two tablespoons mustard seed, a little cayenne pepper, one gallon vinegar. Simmer slowly two or three hours.

Mustard Pickles.

Two quarts cucumbers, two quarts green tomatoes, two quarts small onions, two quarts cauliflower; soak in a weak brine over night, drain, and cook each separately till tender. For the paste: one gallon vinegar, one large cup flour, one pound mustard, three cups sugar; stir the paste until it boils, then pour it over the vegetables. Put in jars, keep covered tightly.

Pickled Cucumbers.

Wash and wipe the cucumbers and place in stone jars. To one gallon of the best cider vinegar, add one teacup salt, two red peppers cut fine, one-fourth pound white mustard seed, one-fourth ounce ginger-root, a piece of alum the size of a butternut, teacup of horscradish root not grated, two onions cut in several pieces, cloves or other spices may be added if desired. Bring the ingredients to a boil, pour over the cucumbers, cover closely and they are finished.

Pickled Eggs.

Put a few black pepper kernels and two small cayenne peppers into enough cider vinegar to cover the eggs; break up some sticks of cinnamon and put into a thin piece of muslin with a few whole cloves and allspice, tie them up and put into the vinegar; while this is cooking boil your eggs ten minutes, take out and put in cold water, when cold peel and put in a small jar and pour the hot vinegar over them; leave the bag of spices in the vinegar. When cold cover with cloth first, then with paper tied over them. In a week they will be ready for use. Serve in slices.

Tomato Catsup.

Take tomatoes when fully ripe, wash and slice them, put into a jar in alternate layers of tomatoes and salt, let them stand four days stirring each day to prevent fermentation. On the fifth day put into a porcelain kettle, boil until reduced to half. To each quart add one teaspoon of mace, two of cloves, two of black pepper, half teaspoon cayenne if liked. Bottle and cork tight.

Currant Catsup.

Five pounds currants freed from stems, five cups brown sugar, one pint vinegar, one tablespoon each of cloves and cinnamon, one teaspoon salt. Boil one hour; keep in sealed jars in a cool place.

Pepper Mangoes.

Take large green peppers, cut a slit in the side, take out the seeds and let stand in strong salt brine twenty-four hours; take out and stuff with chopped cabbage, season with salt, mustard seed and celery seed; tie together again, put in stone jar and cover with scalded vinegar. Let stand at least one month.

CAKE-MAKING.

Table of Weights and Measures.

1 quart flour	1 pound.
2 cups butter	1 pound.
2 cups granulated sugar	1 pound.
2 cups heaping powdered sugar	1 pound.
1 pint of finely chopped meat packed solidly	1 pound.

The cup used for these measures must hold half pint.

Liquids.

4 tablespoons	equal 1 wine glass or half gill.
8 tablespoons	equal 1 gill.
16 tablespoons	equal ½ pint.
12 tablespoons	equal 1 teacup.
16 tablespoons	equal 1 coffee-cup.
2 gills	equal ½ pint.
2 pints	equal 1 quart.
4 quarts	equal 1 gallon.

In cake-making use only the best materials. Eggs will beat more quickly if placed in cold water a short time. Grease cake pans with lard; line the bottom and sides of cake tins with paper. Measure the flour before sifting unless otherwise stated; sift the baking powder with part of the flour two or three times.

I can very well recommend the Snow Flake baking powder as it makes a very close grained cake, which has the advantage over many others. For measuring ingredients use half pint cups.

In mixing cake the butter and sugar should be beaten together until they look like cream; use a wooden spoon. Beat the eggs, yolks and whites separately and add the strained yolks to the butter and sugar, then the whites; next add half the milk and when this is well mixed, half the flour, then rest of the milk and the remainder of the flour containing the baking powder; flavor. This is a good rule to follow unless otherwise directed.

In making fruit cake put in the spices after the butter and sugar have been beaten to a cream, mix well; add the fruit after the cake is all mixed.

To mix velvet sponge cake beat the whites of eggs and put into bowl in which you make the cake, then put in the strained and beaten yolks and beat lightly together; add the sugar and beat thoroughly, now put in part of the flour, beating well, stir in half of the boiling water then add the rest of the flour containing baking powder beating gently and flavor, adding lastly the balance of the hot water. Bake immediately.

In mixing sponge cake proceed as above leaving out the water, being careful to beat in gently the flour containing baking powder.

Too much care cannot be given to the preparation of the oven. The oven may be tested by holding the hand inside for twenty or twenty-five seconds, if the heat can be borne that length of time the oven is in good order. When placed in the stove the cake should be covered with a brown paper cap; care should be taken not to remove cake from the oven till done. Test with a knitting needle, if the dough does not adhere it is done.

A few Rules to Test Oven Heat.

Try the oven every ten minutes with a piece of white paper; if too hot the paper will blaze up or blacken. When the paper becomes a dark brown the oven is fit for small pastry; when light brown the color of really nice pastry it is ready for tarts, etc.; when the paper turns dark yellow you can bake bread, large meat pies or large pound cakes, while if it is just tinged, the oven is fit for sponge cake, meringues, etc.

LOAF CAKES.

Lady Cake No. 1.

Two cups white sugar, three cups flour, three-fourths cup butter, whipped whites of ten eggs; flavor with extract almond; one and one-half teaspoons Snow Flake baking powder. Bake in square but not very deep tins. Flavor the frosting with one-half teaspoon extract vanilla.

Lady Cake No. 2.

Two cups sugar, whites of seven eggs, a scant cup butter, one cup sweet milk, one cup corn starch, two cups flour, two tea spoons Snow Flake baking powder. Flavor with one teaspoon extract almond.

White Delicate Cake.

Two cups granulated sugar, one-half cup butter, one cup cold water, three cups flour, two teaspoons corn starch, one tablespoon good whiskey, two teaspoons Snow Flake baking powder. The whites of four or five eggs, flavor with one teaspoon extract vanilla, lemon or almond.

Angels Food.

One and half tumblers of pulverized sugar, one tumbler of flour, sift before measuring, whites thirteen eggs; sift flour and sugar thirteen times, oftener the better; teaspoon lemon and vanilla together, tablespoon fresh cream tartar. Bake sixty minutes. Alice C.

Brides' Cake

Half cup butter, one and half cups sugar, half cup milk, whites of six eggs, two and half cups flour, one and a half teaspoons Snow Flake baking powder. Flavor with twenty drops extract almond. If you wish the cake larger double the quantity of ingredients.

Angel Cake.

Whites of eleven eggs, one and half tumblers granulated sugar, one tumbler flour, half teaspoon extract vanilla. Beat the whites very stiff in a large platter; sift sugar four times, the last time sift in one teaspoon cream tartar. Add the sugar gradually, to the beaten whites, beating constantly until it is all mixed in, then add the vanilla. Sift in the flour and stir as lightly as possible, bake about forty minutes in a moderate oven, when done turn upside down and let cool; then run a knife round the edge and tube until it will slip out. The tumbler to hold a little more than two gills; ice when cool. Tins made purposly for this cake can be obtained.

Marble Cake.

White Part.—One cup white sugar, half cup butter, half cup milk, whites of three eggs, one and half teaspoons Snow Flake baking powder, two cups flour; flavor to taste.

Dark Part.—Half cup brown sugar, quarter cup butter, half cup molasses, quarter cup milk, half nutmeg, one teaspoon cinnamon, quarter teaspoon cloves, yolks of three eggs, two cups flour, one and half teaspoon baking powder. Put in cake pan; the dark and light batter in alternate tablespoons.

Cup Cake.

One cup butter, two of sugar, three and half cups flour,

two teaspoons Snow Flake baking powder, one cup milk, four eggs. Flavor with grated nutmeg.

Butter-Cup Cake.

Yolks three eggs, half cup butter, one cup sugar, one and half cups flour, one even teaspoon Snow Flake baking powder, one teaspoon vanilla.

Daisy Cake.

Whites three eggs, half cup butter, one cup sugar, one and half cups flour, one even teaspoon Snow Flake baking powder, one teaspoon extract lemon. These two cakes should be made at the same time; the white cake may be frosted with yellow frosting and the butter cup cake with white frosting for which see rules for frosting.

Columbian Pound Cake 1892.

One and half cups butter, two cups granulated sugar, nine eggs, four cups flour, one wine glass of brandy, one teaspoon extract lemon, two teaspoons Snow Flake baking powder sifted three times with the flour. Bake from sixty to seventy minutes in moderate oven.

Annie's Pound Cake.

Two cups sugar, one and a quarter cups butter, seven eggs, half cup water, half cup brandy or whiskey, one teaspoon extract lemon, four cups flour, two teaspoons Snow Flake baking powder sifted with the flour three times.

White Fruit Cake.

One cup butter, two cups white sugar, one cup milk, three and half cups flour, save out little to flour the fruit, two teaspoons Snow Flake baking powder sifted with part of the flour, whites of seven eggs; beat altogether before adding the fruit. Take two cups seeded and chopped raisins, two of chopped figs, one cup blanched almonds, half cup citron, little cocoanut if desired. Flavor with lemon. Bake slowly in moderate oven.

Fruit Cake.—No. 1.

One cup butter, two and half cups sugar, six eggs, one and half nutmegs, one teaspoon cloves, one of extract vanilla, one tablespoon cinnamon, four tablespoons molasses, one wine glass of brandy, one of sherry wine, four cups flour, take out little for flouring fruit, two tablespoons of currant jelly or grape jam, five cups seeded raisins, one cup currants, one cup sliced citron, one cup shell bark kernels, roll rather fine. Dissolve soda the size of a large pea in two or three teaspoons warm coffee, stir this into the molasses and add to the batter just before putting in the fruit. When all mixed bake two hours in a moderate oven.

Fruit Cake.—No. 2.

Two scant cups butter, three cups brown sugar, six eggs, four cups seeded raisins, one cup currants, half cup citron, half cup molasses, half cup sour milk, half nutmeg, one tablespoon ground cinnamon, one teaspoon cloves, one teaspoon mace, one wine glass good whiskey, four cups sifted flour, one level teaspoon soda dissolved in the sour milk, two tablespoons flour for mixing fruit. A lady says: "Best recipe of all."

Imperial Cake.

Two cups sugar, one and half cups butter, four cups flour with two teaspoons Snow Flake baking powder, one cup blanched almonds chopped fine, two cups seeded raisins, one cup citron sliced fine, one nutmeg, one wine glass whiskey or brandy. This cake will keep for months.

Walnut Cake.

One and half cups sugar, half cup butter, half cup milk, three eggs, one and half teaspoon Snow Flake baking powder, two cups flour, one cup walnut meats, vanilla flavoring. Add the nut meats broken very fine, last.

Sponge Cake.

Two cups sugar, two cups flour, ten eggs, two teaspoons Snow Flake baking powder, one teaspoon extract lemon; bake in deep pan from thirty to thirty-five minutes.

Velvet Sponge.

Four eggs, two cups sugar little scant, two cups flour, two teaspoons Snow Flake baking powder, seven table-spoons boiling water; flavor with teaspoon extract lemon, or vanilla. Excellent.

Mary's Drop Sponge Cake.

One cup sugar, one cup flour, four eggs, one small tea-spoon Snow Flake baking powder, beat the yolks and sugar together; add the whites and flavoring to taste. For Lady Fingers they are baked in long narrow strips and are nice frosted with chocolate frosting.

Cream Sponge Cake.

Two cups sugar, one of cream, two of flour, four eggs, one teaspoon Snow Flake baking powder and teaspoon extract lemon.

LAYER CAKES.

Ice Cream Cake No. 1..

Half cup butter, two cups sugar, one cup milk, three cups flour, two teaspoons cornstarch, two teaspoons Snow Flake baking powder, whites of five eggs, twenty drops extract almond. Bake in two long pans. Filling—boil three cups sugar in twelve tablespoons water, until it will gum in cold water; then pour it slowly over the beaten whites of three eggs, beating all the time. Flavor with half teaspoon extract vanilla; spread while warm between. Make the top layer the thickest.

Ice Cream Cake No. 2.

Make white cake and bake in jelly cake tins. Filling— One pint whipped cream, sweeten and flavor to taste, chop fine two cups blanched almonds, stir in the cream and put in thick layers, between the cake.

Marshmallow Cake.

Half cup butter, two cups powdered sugar, three cups sifted flour, two teaspoons Snow Flake baking powder, half cup milk, whites of five eggs, half teaspoon vanilla. Bake in jelly cake tins. Filling—Make boiled icing of one cup sugar, five tablespoons water and the beaten whites of two eggs. Put in a moderate oven, quarter pound marshmallows, when thoroughly softened (care must be taken they do not brown) beat them into the icing. The marshmallows should be added before the icing cools. Use no flavoring. Spread between layers, plain icing for the top.

M. P. A., Mt. Vernon, Ohio.

English Walnut.

Three eggs, four tablespoons butter, two cups sugar,

one cup milk, three of flour, two teaspoons Snow Flake baking powder, flavor to taste; bake in three layers. Frosting—Four whites of eggs, nine teaspoons pulverized sugar, to each white beat about five minutes, one pound English walnuts, save out enough whole half pieces to put on top and take the rest and chop fine and put in two-thirds of the icing, put between layers. This frosting is also nice put in white cake if preferred. Hickory nuts can be used.

Fig Cake.

White Part.—Two cups sugar, two-thirds cup butter, two-thirds cup milk, three cups sifted flour, two teaspoons Snow Flake baking powder, whites of eight eggs, mix and bake in two layers.

Yellow Part.—One cup sugar, half cup butter, half cup milk, yolks of seven eggs and one whole one, one and half cups flour, one teaspoon baking powder; flavor with cinnamon. Put half the yellow batter into a pan corresponding to the pans the white cakes were baked in, put over this batter a layer of figs cut in halves. Dust a little flour over, put in rest of the batter and bake. When done put the gold cake between the two white layers with a little icing between each of the layers, ice the whole cake if desired.

White Mountain Cake.

Two cups sugar, whites eight eggs, two-thirds cup butter, half cup milk, one cup cornstarch, one cup flour, one and half teaspoons Snow Flake baking powder, one teaspoon extract lemon. Bake in jelly cake tins. Frosting— Two cups grated cocoanut steeped in half cup new milk until tender; beat whites of four eggs, one cup white sugar, one tablespoon cornstarch; add the steeped cocoanut, stir altogether and spread over the cakes; pile up alternately cocoanut and cakes until the cakes are all used, and last spread the remaining cocoanut over the top and sides of the cake and sprinkle dry cocoanut over all.

Mrs. H. D. McC., Ft. Madison, Iowa.

Cream Cake.

One and half cups pulverized sugar, half cup butter, half small cup of milk, whites of five eggs beaten stiff, two good cups flour, two small teaspoons Snow Flake baking powder. Flavor with half teaspoon vanilla. Bake in pie tins and cut in two for filling.

Filling.—One large cup cream, small tablespoon cornstarch, one tablespoon sugar, cooked in water. When cool and done add half cup cream beaten stiff, any flavoring; stir well and put between cake. For the frosting make boiled icing of one cup sugar and one egg.

Chocolate Cake.

Two cups sugar, one of butter, the yolks of five eggs and whites of two, one cup milk, three and half cups flour, two teaspoons Snow Flake baking powder; flavor to taste.

Mixture for Filling.—The whites of three eggs, one and half cups sugar, three tablespoons grated chocolate, one teaspoon extract vanilla. Beat well and spread between the layers and on top.

Maple Sugar Cake.

Two cups brown sugar, half cup butter, half cup milk, two and half cups flour, one teaspoon Snow Flake baking powder, three eggs.

Filling.—Six tablespoons shaved maple sugar; add very little water and boil until it strings from spoon; when cool add the white of one egg whipped and one or two tablespoons chocolate; use this between the layers.

Neapolitan Cake.

White Part.—Two cups sugar, two tablespoons butter, two cups flour, whites six eggs, two teaspoons Snow Flake baking powder, one grated cocoanut, one cup citron chopped fine, two cups blanched almonds cut in very thin slices. Flavor with one teaspoon extract almond. Bake in three jelly cake pans.

Dark Part.—One cup sugar, half cup butter, two cups flour, two teaspoons baking powder, yolks six eggs; add two cups seeded raisins, half cup each citron and figs, one teaspoon cloves, one nutmeg, one wine glass of good whiskey. Bake in jelly pans.

Icing.—Three cups sugar, six tablespoons hot water, boil till brittle and stir in the whites of three eggs, add half teacup each of minced almonds and grated cocoanut, spread alternately on the dark and white cake and put together. Ice the top with plain icing. This is elegant.

Lemon Sponge Cake.

Six eggs, three cups sugar, four cups sifted flour, two teaspoons Snow Flake baking powder, one cup cold water, one lemon. Mix quickly; bake in jelly pans, six layers.

Filling.—Two grated lemons, juice and rind, half cup butter, two cups sugar and the whites of six eggs, let boil a few minutes, spread when cool. Orange can be used the same way.

Almond Sponge Cake.

Whites of ten eggs, one goblet of flour, one and half goblets sugar, one teaspoon cream tartar. Bake in two jelly cake tins. Sift the sugar once; flour and cream tartar four times. For the custard.—One cup cream or milk; boil it and stir in three well beaten yolks, two

6

tablespoons sugar, one teaspoon cornstarch dissolved in cold milk. Boil until thick; when cool add one cup of blanched almonds chopped fine, saving out two dozen to put on top. After putting the cream between the cakes ice the top with one egg, a small cup of sugar and a very little bitter almond, then ornament with whole almonds.

Roll Jelly Cake.

Four eggs, one cup sugar, one cup flour, one teaspoon Snow Flake baking powder, small teaspoon extract lemon. This will make two cakes, spread thin on long tins. As soon as baked turn from tins and spread over jelly, roll immediately in damp cloth.

SMALL CAKES.

Aunt-Eliza's Jumbles No. 1.

Half cup lard, half cup butter, two cups sugar, beat to a cream, add the beaten yolks of three eggs, into this grate a little nutmeg, add to this one cup sour milk in which one teaspoon soda has been dissolved. Stir in the beaten whites of eggs, then work in sufficient flour to make a soft dough, it may take six cups, roll out and cut with cake cutter.

Jumbles No. 2.

One cup butter, two cups sugar, beaten to a cream, four eggs, three-quarters cup sweet milk, one teaspoon extract vanilla, three teaspoons Snow Flake baking powder. Flour enough to make a soft dough, roll thin and bake in hot oven.

Spiced Gingerbread.

One cup sugar, one cup molasses, three-fourths cup

butter, two eggs, two teaspoons Snow Flake Baking powder, half cup coffee, two teaspoons extract ginger, two teaspoons cinnamon, one of cloves. Flour for rather a stiff batter.   Mabel W.

Gingerbread of 1827.

One cup sugar, one cup molasses, half cup lard, three eggs, small teaspoon cloves, one teaspoon extract of ginger, one teaspoon soda dissolved in half cup warm coffee, and flour to made as thick as pound cake.

Sponge Gingerbread.

One cup molasses, one cup brown sugar, one cup sour milk, two eggs, half cup lard, one teaspoon extract of ginger, one teaspoon soda dissolved in the milk, three and a half to four cups flour.

Ginger Cakes.

Three eggs, one and half cups molasses, one and half cups sugar, half cup lard, half cup sour milk, a good teaspoon soda dissolved in the milk, two teaspoons extract of ginger; work well with sufficient flour to roll out; cut in cakes.

Ginger Snaps.

One large cup butter and lard mixed, one coffee cup sugar, one cup molasses, half cup water, one tablespoon ginger, one of cinnamon, one teaspoon cloves, one teaspoon soda dissolved in hot water. Flour for pretty stiff dough. Roll out thin.

Doughnuts No. 1.

One and half small tea-cups butter, four cups light brown sugar, four eggs beaten separately, one large pint sour milk, one teaspoon soda dissolved in the milk, a little grated nutmeg. Mix like pound cake.

Mrs. S. S., St. Paul.

Doughnuts No. 2.

Two cups sugar, two teaspoons butter, three eggs, one cup sour milk, teaspoon soda, spice to taste.   Flour to roll.

Jimmy's Doughnuts.

One and half cups sugar, one tablespoon butter, one cup milk, two eggs, one and half teaspoons Snow Flake baking powder, little nutmeg.   Flour to roll; fry in hot lard. These are nice.

Ned's Doughnuts.

One cup sugar, two tablespoons butter, three eggs, two teaspoons Snow Flake baking powder, one cup milk, nutmeg to taste.

FILLINGS FOR CAKES.

Fruit Filling.

Four tablespoons of very fine chopped citron, four tablespoons of finely chopped seeded raisins, half cup blanched almonds chopped fine, also two tablespoons finely chopped figs.   Beat the whites of three eggs to a stiff froth adding half cup sugar, then mix into this the whole of the chopped ingredients.   Put it between the layers of cake when the cake is hot so that it will cook the egg a little.   This will be found delicious.

Peach Cream Filling.

Cut peaches in thin slices, or chop; prepare cream by whipping and sweetening.   Put a layer of peaches between layers of cake and pour cream over each layer and over the top. Bananas, strawberries and other fruits may be used in the same way; mashing strawberries and sprinkling with powdered sugar.

Chocolate Filling.

Bakers chocolate square, yolks two eggs, one cup sugar, one-third cup boiled milk. Stir the chocolate and sugar into the boiling milk, then add the eggs well beaten; simmer ten minutes. Flavor with extract vanilla. Let it cool before using.

Cream Filling.

One pint cream beaten stiff, six tablespoons sugar, whites of two eggs beaten stiff; mix. Flavor with vanilla.

ICINGS AND SAUCES FOR CAKES AND PUDDING. ICE CREAM.

Boiled Icing.—No. 1.

Boil one cup granulated sugar with four tablespoons hot water until it drops from the spoon in threads, have ready the beaten white of one egg and pour the syrup over it slowly, beating all the time; flavor. Put on cake while warm.

Boiled Icing.—No. 2.

Dissolve two cups sugar in three tablespoons water and boil until brittle. Beat the whites of four eggs, pour over the hot sugar and stir; flavor and use while hot.

Chocolate Icing.

Melt three tablespoons chocolate dissolve in little water, boil in two cups sugar, in which stir the whites of three eggs, well beaten. Flavor with vanilla to taste.

Icing for Cake.

To the white of one egg, beaten, stir six tablespoons powdered sugar. Cake must be cold before being used.

Almond Icing.

Whites of three eggs beaten to a froth, one cup blanched almonds chopped fine, ten tablespoons pulverized sugar. Flavor with bitter almonds.

Cocoanut Icing.

Whites of three eggs, twelve tablespoons sugar, one grated cocoanut. Beat sugar and eggs together; spread on the cake and sprinkle the cocoanut over thickly This will make a whiter frosting than stirring in the cocoanut.

Orange Icing.

Whites of two eggs, twelve tablespoons sugar, two oranges grated.

Water Icing.

Two cups sugar, add water enough to form a thick paste; beat well; if too thin add more sugar, a pinch of cream tartar.

Yellow Frosting.

Yolk of one egg, ten tablespoons sugar cr enough to stiffen. Flavor with vanilla.

Pudding Sauce.—No. 1.

Whites two eggs, two-thirds cup sugar, beaten together; add teacup boiling milk. Flavor to taste.

Pudding Sauce.—No. 2.

Mix the yolks of four eggs, four tablespoons sugar, one of flour, two cups milk; set on fire and stir until thick. Flavor with nutmeg.

Cold Sauce.

One cup butter, one cup sugar, beaten to a froth. Flavor to suit taste.

Brandy Sauce.

Beat the yolks of five eggs with one cup sugar until light, add quarter cup butter that has been beaten to a cream, add one pint boiling water; stir until it thickens, take from fire and add half cup brandy.

Caramel Sauce.

Put one cup sugar in a small frying pan and stir on the fire until a dark brown. Add a cup boiling water and simmer about twenty minutes.

Lemon Sauce.

One large cup sugar, nearly half cup butter, one egg, one lemon, juice and half the grated rind, one nutmeg, three tablespoons boiling water, cream, butter and sugar, beat in the egg whipped lightly, the lemon and nutmeg, beat hard ten minutes; add one spoon at a time boiling water, put in tin pail and set within the uncovered top of tea kettle, which must be kept boiling until the steam heats the sauce very hot, but not to boiling. Stir constantly.

Hard Sauce.

The whipped whites of six eggs, add two cups sugar, half cup creamed butter. Flavor with extract rose or to taste.

Foaming Sauce.

Whites three eggs, melt a tea cup sugar in little water, let boil, stir in one glass of wine and then the eggs.

Wine Sauce.—No. 1.

Ten tablespoons of water, six of sugar, eight of wine, four of butter; stir to a cream then add little boiling water just before wanted for the table.

Wine Sauce.—No. 2.

One cup butter, yolks of two beaten eggs, nine tablespoons of brown sugar, two glasses of wine. Let simmer on fire a short time.

Cream Sauce.

One pint cream, one cup sugar, tablespoon butter, one glass wine. Beat altogether.

Rock Cream.

Boil one cup rice till soft, in milk sweetened with white sugar and pile on a dish, lay on it in different places square pieces of currant jelly. Beat the whites of five eggs with little powdered sugar, flavor with vanilla, add to this when beaten two tablespoons rich cream.

Jelly Cream.

Beat the whites of six eggs to a froth, add gradually six tablespoons powdered sugar, beating not less than thirty minutes, then beat in one cup jelly, cut in small pieces, serve in glass dishes.

Whipped Cream.

One pint sweet cream, sweetened to taste, one teaspoon vanilla or other flavoring. Put the cream in a bowl and beat with a wheel egg beater until thick; then sweeten and flavor, the cream will beat better if cold. The whites of three eggs beaten to a stiff froth, may be added. This makes a lovely dessert. Different jellies or fruit may be served with it.

Frosted Custard.

Make custard, let cool and pile on it, cocoanut grated and powdered sugar. Eat with lemon jelly cake.

Substitute for Cream.

Boil three-fourths pint sweet milk, beat the yolk of one egg and a level teaspoon flour, with sugar enough to make the cream very sweet; when the milk boils stir this into it and let it cool. Flavor to taste. This is almost as good as rich cream for puddings.

Substitute for Cream for Coffee.

Beat well the yolks of two eggs and stir them into one pint milk, add a little sugar about tablespoon; place over fire stirring in one direction until it is the consistency of cream. After it is cold add some cream if you have it.

Ice Cream.—No. 1.

Take three quarts milk, one quart cream, four cups sugar, six eggs; scald the milk in a kettle of water, add one tablespoon flour to each quart of milk; yolks of the eggs well beaten and the sugar; when cold the whites of the eggs whipped to a froth, also cream beaten. Strain the whole and flavor to taste.

Ice Cream.—No. 2.

Take four quarts cream, four cups sugar, stir well together, add half teaspoon bitter almonds and extract vanilla to taste. Strain and freeze.

Ice Cream.—No. 3.

One quart cream, one cup sugar, whites of five eggs, beat altogether; flavor with vanilla and freeze.

Strawberry Ice Cream.

Two quarts cream, two of ripe strawberries and three cups sugar; let stand two hours and strain, add another cup sugar then freeze.

Peach Ice Cream.

Take ripe peaches, to each quart after being mashed, add one pint cream, one pint milk, half box gelatine, dissolved and mixed in. Sweeten to taste and freeze.

Caramel Ice Cream.

Put two pints of brown sugar in a skillet and stir until dissolved, mix in one pint boiling milk, cool and strain, pour it in two quarts cream. Some like little vanilla flavoring.

Banana Ice Cream.

One quart cream, six bananas, one and half cups sugar, the beaten yolks of three eggs, one pint water. Boil the sugar and water together twenty minutes, rub the bananas through a seive and add to the boiling syrup, add also the yolks of eggs and cook for six minutes, stirring all the time. Take from the fire and place in a pan of cold water, beat the mixture ten minutes. If cold at that length of time, add the cream and freeze.   For May.

BOILED, BAKED AND STEAMED PUDDING.

Quick Puff Pudding.

Sift together, one pint flour, one heaping teaspoon Snow Flake baking powder, a little salt, add milk enough to make a stiff batter. Place in a steamer, five well greased cups, put in each one a spoonful of batter, then one of berries, apples or any other sauce convenient, cover with another spoonful batter, steam half hour. Eat with the following sauce.

Sauce—To one pint boiling water add one tea cup sugar, tablespoon butter, pinch salt, tablespoon cornstarch, dissolved in cold water, flavor with nutmeg or vanilla and boil half hour.

Baked Custard.

One quart milk, six eggs, one cup sugar, vanilla to taste. Boil the milk; when nearly cool add the sugar, eggs and flavoring. Bake in pudding dish in a slow oven till done. Try it by slipping a spoon handle into the edge; If the milk does not follow the spoon the custard is set and remove at once from the oven.   J. W. C.

Rice Pudding.

Boil one and half cups rice, then add three cups milk, three fourths cup sugar, half glass wine, quarter cup butter, half cup seeded raisins, half of sliced citron.

Beat five eggs, leave out the whites of three and mix in; pour over half cup brandy, put in pan and bake one hour. Make a meringue of the three whites whipped to a froth, and three tablespoons sugar flavored with nutmeg. Eat without sauce.

Delicious Pudding.

One quart milk, one pint bread crumbs, one cup white sugar, yolks of four eggs, small piece of butter, a little salt. Bake as a custard, cover with any kind of fruit, then beat the whites to a cream, add tablespoon sugar, spread over and brown.

Orange Pudding.

Pare and slice four large oranges, take out the seeds, put in bottom of pudding dish with a cup of sugar; boil one pint of milk, and stir in two tablespoons cornstarch wet with a little cold milk; add yolks of two eggs, beaten with half cup of sugar; boil one minute and pour over oranges. Make a meringue of whites of two eggs, three tablespoons powdered sugar; brown slightly. If you want a large pudding double the quantity.

Cocoanut Pudding.

One cup sugar, five eggs, one quart milk, one cocoanut grated. Boil the milk and add the eggs, well beaten and the sugar and cocoanut. Bake till set; if more convenient you can use one and half cups dessicated cocoanut and half cup sugar.

Prune Pudding.

Stew one and half pounds prunes, take out the seeds and chop rather fine. Beat the whites of six eggs, add one cup white sugar, gradually beating all the time, then stir in the chopped prunes, bake twenty minutes. Serve cold with whipped cream and wine. Delicious.

Peach Pudding.

Fill a pudding dish with whole peaches pared, pour over them, two cups water, cover closely and bake until peaches are tender, then drain off the juice from the peaches, let stand until cool. Add to the juice one pint milk, four well beaten eggs, a small cup of flour with one teaspoon Snow Flake baking powder mixed in it, one cup sugar, one tablespoon melted butter and a little salt. Beat well three or four minutes and pour over peaches, bake until a rich brown. Serve with cream.

Peach Tapioca Pudding.

One dozen peaches, one cup tapioca, one cup white sugar. Soak tapioca in cold water three hours; put on the stove until it boils. Add the sugar, pare and slice the peaches, sprinkle with sugar and pour the tapioca over them. Bake slowly one hour. Serve with cream.

Cottage Pudding.

One cup sugar, one of milk, one tablespoon butter, two eggs, one and half teaspoons Snow Flake baking powder; bake in one loaf in buttered tin. Sauce:—One cup sugar, half cup butter, half cup wine, one egg, cream, butter and sugar; add the egg and beat very light.

Graham Pudding.

One cup sugar, one cup sweet milk, one cup chopped raisins, two scant cups Graham flour, one egg, one and half teaspoons Snow Flake baking powder, nutmeg, one teaspoon salt. Steam three hours; serve with lemon sauce.

Plum Pudding.—No. 1.

Nine eggs, three cups stoned raisins, one cup currants, half cup citron, cut fine; flour the fruit; one tablespoon brown sugar, three cups sweet milk, flour to make thick batter, two and half teaspoons Snow Flake baking powder, a little salt, half nutmeg, two tablespoons chopped suet. Boil in pudding bag five hours and leave space of six inches to swell. Before putting mixture into the bag rinse it in cold water and flour well inside. When pudding is done plunge into cold water for an instant, then remove the cloth. Serve with brandy sauce.

Plum Pudding.—No. 2.

Four eggs, one cup chopped suet, two cups seeded raisins, one cup currants, half cup sugar, two and half cups flour, one cup sweet milk, one and half teaspoons Snow Flake baking powder, pinch of salt, one teaspoon cinnamon, quarter teaspoon cloves, half nutmeg grated. Put all the ingredients in a bowl with the yolks of eggs well beaten. Add part of the whites and flour alternately.

Cream Pudding.

One pint sour cream, one pint stoned raisins, half cup citron, three well beaten eggs, half nutmeg, pinch of salt, one level teaspoon soda dissolved in the cream, one cup brown sugar, flour to make stiff batter, three tablespoons good whiskey. Boil steadily one and half hours. Serve with brandy sauce.

Harry's Cherry Pudding.

Four eggs, half cup butter, one pint milk, flour to make thick batter, one and half teaspoons Snow Flake baking powder, half teaspoon salt, one cup stoned cherries. Boil in pudding bag and eat with sauce.

Baked Dumplings.

One quart flour, two teaspoons Snow Flake baking powder, half teaspoon salt, mixed together. Add one large tablespoon butter and lard mixed and enough sweet milk or water to make a soft dough, roll out into thin sheets, Pare and quarter some good tart apples. Put each quarter on a square of dough, sprinkle over it sugar and press the edges together firmly. Place in a deep pan and put a bit of butter on each. Fill the pan with water (boiling) just leaving top of dumplings uncovered. Serve with sweetened cream or hard sauce. These are little beauties.

Apple Pudding.

One quart chopped apples, one pint flour, in which has been sifted one heaping teaspoon Snow Flake baking powder, half teaspoon salt, one pint new milk, four eggs. Bake and serve with sauce.

Flour Pudding.

One pint milk, four eggs, whites and yolks beaten separately, two even cups of flour, one and half teaspoons Snow Flake baking powder, half teaspoon salt; bake in buttered dish three-quarters of an hour. Serve as soon as it is taken from oven, eat with sweetened cream and nutmeg.

Orange Rolly Pooly.

Make a light paste as for apple dumplings, roll out in a long sheet and lay sweet oranges peeled, sliced and seeded thickly all over it, sprinkle with white sugar and roll up closely, folding down the ends to secure the syrup. Boil in a pudding cloth one and half hours. Eat with lemon sauce.

A Summer Day Dessert.

Slice half dozen bananas; pour over them the juice of one lemon, well sweetened with pulverized sugar.

May.

Creamed Bananas.

Slice the bananas and strew with sugar, whip one cup of cream very light, whip the white of an egg to stiff froth. Put egg and cream together with a tablespoon sugar; pour over the bananas. Peaches are nice served the same way.

7

PUFF PASTES AND PIES.

Puff Paste.

Four cups sifted flour, two of butter folded in a cloth and pressed to remove the moisture; sift the flour on a board in the centre, squeeze the juice of a lemon and add the beaten yolk of an egg, stir and pour in ice water until the paste is stiff; roll out smooth, spread the butter over half the paste, lay the other half over and put on ice fifteen minutes, then roll out and double in three parts, on which spread butter and fold over; handle as little as possible and keep on ice until ready to use.

Plain Pie Crust.

Four cups flour, one cup lard, half teaspoon salt, one small teaspoon Snow Flake baking powder, water to make into stiff dough.

Rule for an Under Crust.

A good rule for pie requiring only an under crust: three large tablespoons of flour sifted, rubbing into it a large tablespoon of cold butter or part butter and part lard and a pinch of salt, mixing with cold water enough to form a smooth paste and rolled quite thin.

An easy Method for One Pie.

One heaping cup flour, half teaspoon Snow Flake baking powder, half teaspoon salt, quarter cup lard, quarter cup butter; mix salt with flour and rub in lard; mix stiff with cold water, roll out; put the butter on the paste in pieces the size of beans and sprinkle with flour. Fold over and roll to fit the plate. For Emma.

Lemon Pie.—No. 1.

Juice and rind of two lemons, two cups sugar, six eggs, two cups milk, two tablespoons flour; smooth the flour in little milk, scald the rest of the milk and add to it the thickening. Beat the yolks of the eggs and sugar together, add these to the milk. Add the grated rind and juice of the lemons. Bake in deep plates lined with undercrust; when done frost with the beaten whites mixed with four tablespoons sugar. Brown the frosting lightly.

Lemon Pie.—No. 2.

Two soda crackers, two lemons, one and half cups sugar, two eggs, one and half cups boiling water. Roll crackers fine, place in bowl, pour on boiling water, cover with plate; when cold add eggs beaten, sugar, grated rind of one, and juice of both lemons. Bake between two crusts in a quick oven twenty-five minutes.

Cream Pie—No. 1.

One pint cream, yolks of three eggs, seven tablespoons sugar, one teaspoon butter, one small teaspoon cornstarch, whites of five eggs and five dessert spoons of powdered sugar for meringue, vanilla flavoring, stir butter and sugar together, beat the cornstarch into the yolks of the eggs until smooth, then stir these two compounds together. Add one teaspoon vanilla and lastly put in the cream, little at a time stirring well between. Fill a shell of puff paste and bake until set over with meringue, return to the oven to bake a delicate brown.

Cream Pie—No. 2.

Two eggs, one cup maple sugar grated and stirred together. Add as much sweet cream as pie dish will hold; bake with one crust.

Orange Pie.

Beat one cup full of powdered sugar and large tablespoon butter together, moisten two even tablespoons of cornstarch with a little cold milk and then stir into it one cup boiling milk, cook and stir one moment, then pour it quickly on the butter and sugar, add the grated yellow rind and the juice of an orange, mix and add one egg well beaten. Peel another large orange, cut into thin slices, and then cut each slice into four pieces, line a pie-plate with light paste and bake in quick oven until done. Stir the orange slices quickly into the custard mixture, fill the baked crust with this, and place in a quick oven a few minutes to brown. While it is browning, beat the whites of two eggs until light, add two tablespoons of powdered sugar and beat until stiff, spread this over the pie, dust thickly with powdered sugar and stand again in the oven until lightly colored.

Custard Pie.

Four eggs, one quart of milk, one tablespoon flour, half cup sugar. Bake with under crust only.

Peach Pie.

Take ripe peaches, wash and wipe, but do not pare them, cut in half, but do not extract stones, place between two crusts with plenty of sugar. The flavor is very fine.

Cream Peach Pie.

Pare ripe peaches and remove the stones, have pie dishes lined with a good paste, fill with the peaches, strew these with sugar and lay the upper crust on lightly, slightly buttering the lower crust around the edge of pie; when the pie is done, lift the cover and pour in a cream made thus: one small cup milk heated, whites of two eggs whipped and stirred into the milk, one tablespoon sugar, half teaspoon cornstarch wet in milk, boil three minutes, put in the hot pie when the cream is cold, replace the crust and set by to cool. Eat fresh.

Gooseberry Pie.

Line pie-tin with paste, sprinkle with little flour, then sugar, fill with gooseberries and make very sweet with sugar on top, cover with crust and bake.

Cocoanut Pie.

One cup white sugar, two cups new milk, three tablespoons flour, one cocoanut grated fine, two eggs, one tablespoon butter; flavor with nutmeg; bake with one crust. For two pies.

Pumpkin Pie.

One pint stewed pumpkin, three eggs; sweeten with sugar to taste, one pint cream or rich milk, a little salt, season with cinnamon and ginger. Bake with one crust.

Cracker Pie.

One lemon, one cup chopped raisins, one of water, one cup rolled crackers, scald the raisins, add one cup sugar and bake in puff paste.

Mince Pie.

Take one and half pints chopped boiled meat, two and a half pints chopped apples, one and half pints of sugar, three-fourths of a pint of vinegar, half pint of broth in which the meat was boiled, a large half pint raw beef suet finely chopped, half pint brandy, two cups of seeded raisins, five teaspoons ground cinnamon and three-fourths tea-spoon ground cloves; mix all well together. It is well only to put in half the brandy when mixing then add one or two tablespoons in each pie just before it is baked. For six pies.

CUSTARDS BOILED.

Boiled Custard.

One quart new milk, six eggs, one cup sugar, one tea-spoon vanilla. Heat the milk boiling hot, beat the sugar and eggs, pour the boiling milk over them, and return to the fire, let boil, stir to keep from burning, when thick pour in a bowl to cool. Fill custard cups and cover with meringue made by whipping the whites of three eggs with currant jelly.

Sabyllon.

Yolks of ten eggs or more, four tablespoons sherry wine to an egg, two tablespoons sugar to an egg. Mix and boil in a double kettle stirring constantly. Serve in small cups with white cake.

Orange Custard.

Peal and cut in small pieces four large oranges, put in a dish with one cup sugar, beat the yolks of three eggs, half cup sugar and two tablespoons cornstarch, pour this in one quart boiling milk, when it thickens, set away to cool, then stir in the oranges; beat the whites to a froth and pour over top. Serve cold.

JELLIES, MARMALADES AND JAMS.

Quince Jelly.

Take one and half dozen quinces, cut in slices and pour cold water over them and let boil till nearly done, then add one dozen sour juicy apples pared and cut up. When quinces and apples are soft, strain through a jelly bag; now measure to each pint of the strained juice one pint of sugar. Set aside the sugar, put the juice on the fire and boil twenty minutes, then add the sugar and boil fifteen or twenty minutes. Put in jelly glasses and cover when cold.

Currant Jelly.—No. 1.

Stem the currants, put in a kettle and mash, add one teacup of water to every gallon of currants; soon as fruit is soft strain. Allow to each pint of juice one pint of sugar, boil the juice twenty minutes then stir in the sugar and boil twenty minutes. This jelly keeps any length of time; the water prevents it from being so strong.

Currant Jelly.—No. 2.

Wash currants, mash in a porcelain dish, squeeze through jelly bag, rinse out bag, run the juice through again without squeezing, then to every pint of juice, add one pint sugar; while boiling skim and boil twenty minutes. An excellent jelly is made by taking one-third currants, two-thirds red raspberries and proceeding as above.

Blackberry, Strawberry or Raspberry Jelly.

Crush the berries, strain the juice with one pint sugar to a pint of juice, boil.

Cranberry Jelly.

Put cranberries in a kettle with very little water, stew till soft, then strain, add one pint of sugar to each pint of jelly. Boil twenty minutes.

Blackberry or Raspberry Jam.

Boil the berries with a very little water, add one pint of currant or plum juice to a gallon of berries, when thoroughly done, add one pint of sugar to every pint of fruit; boil until thick. If tart juice is not used in the berries, take only three quarters pint of sugar to one pint of fruit.

Quince Marmalade.

Take equal quantities of quinces and good sour apples, pare and core each, quarter quinces, put in kettle, cover well with water and boil till moderately soft, add apples and cook until all is soft; boil the parings and good cores in separate water until done, strain into fruit; next press the whole through a colander, now measure, and take one pint of sugar to each pint of fruit, return to the fire and boil slowly half an hour, then stir in sugar and boil one hour, moderately. Put in glass jars. You will find this excellent. Many persons do not boil their fruit long enough to keep well.

Peach Marmalade.

Take the fruit, wipe and cut out defects, put in a kettle

and cover with water, and let boil gently until soft, then remove from fire, take out the seeds and pass the fruit through a colander, then measure; to each pint of fruit take one pint of sugar, return fruit to the fire, boil gently half an hour, then add the sugar and boil from three-quarters to an hour. Put in small glass or stone jars, cover with three thicknesses of white paper, the first dipped in brandy or whiskey, sprinkle thickly on top layer with sugar to prevent moulding. Cover the whole tightly. This is very fine.

DESSERTS.

Banana Pudding.

Half box gelatine, two cups sugar, one quart milk, five bananas, desolve gelatine in cup cold water, thin the gelatine with little hot milk, strain it and add the rest of the milk. Let it simmer upon back of the stove ten minutes, pour into a bowl to cool. Stir the bananas which must be pealed and cut in small pieces into the mixture after it has cooled, (but not stiffened.) Make the day before it is to be used, to give time to harden. Serve with one pint whipped cream, sweetened if desired.

Buttercup Jelly.

Half box gelatine soaked in one cup cold water, heat one pint milk and stir the gelatine in, beat the yolks of three eggs with one heaping cup of sugar and a small pinch of soda. Flavor with teaspoon extract vanilla, boil three minutes, whip the white of an egg and beat into the jelly. Serve with plain or whipped cream.

Snow Custard.

Take half package gelatine, three eggs, two cups sugar and juice of a lemon, soak the gelatine in cup cold water, add one pint boiling water, stir until dissolved, add sugar and lemon juice, beat the whites of the eggs and when the mixture is cold whip in the whites, spoonful. at a time, when stiff put into small cups to mould. When firm turn out, make a custard and pour over; flavor with vanilla.

Strawberry Cream.

One quart strawberries, half package gelatine, one pint cream, one large cup sugar, half cup hot water, mash the berries, then add sugar and mash sugar and berries together, let them stand some time, whip the cream to a froth. Have the gelatine soaked in cold water to cover, strain juice from berries, getting as much as possible through muslin. Now dissolve the gelatine in hot water and strain into berries, place the basin in another of ice water and stir until it begins to thicken, then add whipped cream, put into moulds to harden.

Fruit Jelly.

Pare and slice six oranges very thin and six bananas and orange in layers in a charlotte russe mould. Make a jelly of half.box of gelatine soaked in half pint cold water, then add half pint of boiling water and the juice of three lemons, sweeten to taste, pour this jelly over the fruit when partly cooled and set in cool place to harden.

Strawberry Charlotte.

One quart milk, yolks six eggs, three-quarters cup sugar, flavor to taste, scald the milk, beat the eggs and sugar and stir into the milk and cook until it thickens, taking care that it does not crack. Place slices of sponge cake in a glass dish, then a layer of ripe strawberries, sprinkled with sugar, another layer of cake, then another of berries with sugar. When the custard is cold, pour it over the cake and berries, beat the whites of the eggs to a stiff froth, add sugar and put over the top and decorate with ripe strawberries.

Cornstarch Blanc Mange.

One quart milk, four tablespoon cornstarch wet in little cold water, four eggs well beaten, separately, one cup sugar, vanilla or nutmeg flavoring, quarter teaspoon salt. Heat the milk to boiling, stir in the cornstarch, boil five minutes (in a farina kettle,) then add the yolks with the sugar, boil two minutes longer stirring all the while; remove the mixture from the fire and beat in the whipped whites. Pour into a mould wet with cold water. set in a cold place, eat with sugar and cream.

Bavarian Cream.

Whites of six eggs, beaten very light, one quart whipped cream, half box gelatine soaked one hour in cold water, dissolve in little hot water, flavor with one teaspoon extract vanilla. Beat eggs and cream together, and sugar to sweeten, flavor, then add gelatine; beat until it begins to thicken, and pour into moulds. Serve very cold with cream.

Apple Snow.

Pare, core and bring to a boil in as little water as possible six tart apples, cool and strain, add the well whipped whites of three eggs, sweeten to taste and beat until a dish of snow is the result, flavor to suit taste, serve with sweetened cream or make a custard of the yolks, sugar and one pint rich milk or cream, if at hand. Place in a dish and drop the froth in large flakes.

Charlotte Russe.

One pound lady fingers, one quart sweet cream, three-quarters cup powdered sugar, two teaspoons vanilla, split and trim the cakes and fit neatly in the bottom and sides of two quart moulds; whip the cream to a stiff froth after it has been sweetened and flavored, fill the moulds, lay the cakes closely together on the top and set on ice till needed. The edges of the cake may be moistened with little jelly, that the shape may be more easily retained.

SYRUPS, SHERBETS, ETC.

Sarsaprilla Syrup.

One-half pound of Honduras sarsaparilla, and one ounce of Sassafras bark; boil in two gallons of water four hours, strain and add enough water to make one gallon, then add eight pounds of sugar and five ounces of tartaric acid, mix thoroughly, boil two or three minutes and bottle. Put two tablespoons of the syrup in two-thirds of a glass of ice water, add little soda and drink while foaming.

A Summer Drink.

Three and a half pints of brown sugar, half pint molasses, three pints boiling water, boil these together, skim and add two ounces of tartaric acid; set it away to cool. When cool add one ounce of essence of sassafras, and bottle. A tablespoon or more in a glass of water will make an agreeable drink. Fill the glass two-thirds full and foam it with a little soda.

Currant Shrub.

Heat the currants till soft, and strain; to one quart of juice add two cups sugar, boil fifteen minutes, skimming carefully. Bottle tight or seal in cans.

Lemon Sherbet.

The juice of five lemons, one pint of sugar, one quart water, one tablespoon gelatine, soak the gelatine in little of the water; boil one cup full of the water and dissolve the gelatine in it. Mix together the sugar, water, gelatine and lemon juice, strain and freeze.

Orange Sherbet.

One and half pints of sugar, three pints water, the juice
of ten oranges, boil the sugar and water together, twenty-
five minutes, add the orange juice, strain and freeze.

Strawberry Sherbet.

One and half pints strawberry juice, one pint sugar,
one and half pints water, the juice of two lemons, boil
water and sugar together for twenty minutes, add the
lemon and strawberry juice, strain and freeze.

Frozen Peaches.

One can of peaches, one heaping pint of granulated
sugar, one quart water, two cups whipped cream; boil the
sugar and water together twelve minutes, then add the
peaches and cook twenty minutes longer. Rub through a
sieve and when cool, freeze. When the dasher is taken
out, stir in the whipped cream with large spoon, cover
and set away until serving time. It should stand one
hour.

Orangeade.

Take thin skinned oranges, squeeze the juice through a
sieve, to every pint of juice add three cups sugar, boil it
and skim as long as scum rises, then take it off and bottle.
A little of this makes a delicious drink in a glass of ice
water.

Marshmallows.

Dissolve half pound gumarabic in one pint of water and
add two cups sugar, place over the fire, stirring constantly
until the syrup is dissolved and all of the consistency of
honey, add gradually the whites of four eggs well beaten,
stir the mixture until it becomes somewhat thin and does

not adhere to the fingers. Flavor to taste, pour into a tin slightly dusted with powdered starch, when cool divide into small squares.

Chocolate Caramels.

Two goblets brown sugar, one of water, two tablespoons vinegar, little butter, half cup Baker's chocolate, boil until hard, flavor in tins. Do not stir while boiling.

Hickory Nut Candy.

Three cups sugar, half cup milk, boil ten minutes and stirred white. Then add one and half cups hickory nut meats, turn into a tin, lined with buttered paper. When cold cut in squares.

Sugar Candy.

Six cups sugar, one cup vinegar, one cup water, table-spoon butter put in at the last with one teaspoon soda dissolved in hot water. Boil without stirring half hour or until it crisps in cold water. Pull white with the tips of the fingers. Flavor to taste.

BEVERAGES.

Cocoa.

Six tablespoons cocoa to each pint of water, as much milk as water, sugar to taste; rub cocoa smooth in little cold water. Have ready on fire pint boiling water, stir in grated cocoa paste. Boil twenty minutes, add milk and boil five minutes more, stirring often. Sweeten in cups to suit different tastes.

Coffee.

Take one tablespoon coffee to each person, and one for the pot, one pint water to every tablespoon, mix the coffee with little egg and cold water, put into the coffee pot and pour boiling water over it and boil twenty minutes. To settle coffee pour out a cupful and back to boiler, let stand a moment.

Tea.

Take one teaspoon to each pint boiling water, scald the tea pot and put in the tea, pour little boiling water on it and let stand a few minutes to steep, then pour over sufficient water. If oolong and green tea are used let it simmer a short time.

MISCELLANEOUS.

Meat Cakes.

One cup chopped meat, one onion chopped, one cup bread crumbs, two tablespoons melted butter, six of milk, one egg, salt and pepper; mix well together, roll into round cakes and fry in fat. Use cold veal, beef or pork.

Cousin J. P.

Boiled Flank of Beef.

Wash the flank, salt and pepper it, spread over a dressing, made as for poultry; roll this up and tie firmly, then sew up in a cloth. Lay it on a plate in an iron pot, cover with six quarts boiling water, boil gently six hours. When done remove the cloth but not the twine until the meat is entirely cold. Slice thin for lunch or tea.

Baked Onions.

Slice onions and boil, then place alternately bread crumbs and onions till dish is filled, season with plenty butter, salt and pepper, one cup milk. Bake till brown.

Scalloped Meat.

Almost any kind of meat or poultry may be boiled until tender. Chop and season to taste, place in a dish with alternate layers of bread crumbs and bits of butter. Have the upper layer of crumbs, pour over meat liquor or water enough to moisten, bake till brown.

Rich Nut Cake.

One and half cups sugar, half cup butter, one of milk,

8

half cup cornstarch, three cups flour, two teaspoons Snow
Flake baking powder, whites of six eggs. Flavor with
twenty drops almond, bake in layers. Filling—Make a
rich cream of the yolks of the eggs, one cup milk, one teaspoon cornstarch dissolved in little milk, half cup sugar.
When it is boiled to the consistency of cream set aside to
cool, then mix through it a pound of walnuts broken in
small pieces, spread between layers of cake.

Chocolate Blanc Mange.

Quart of milk, half box of gelatine soaked in one cup
water, four tablespoons Baker's chocolate, grated, rubbed
smooth in little milk, three eggs, extract vanilla to taste.
Heat milk until boiling then add other ingredients, boil
five minutes. Pour into mould. Serve cold with sugar
and cream.

Caramels.

Equal quantities of milk, molasses and Baker's chocolate. Put little butter in sauce pan and boil like candy.

A Mistake

In saying that berries should never be washed, particu-
larly strawberries, which are liable to have more or less
sand. They must be carefully washed in cold water, and
drained immediately. This does not impair the flavor in
the least. Try it.

When buying Chocolate and Cocoa be sure and call for
Walter Baker's.

THINGS TO KNOW.

To prevent juice running from pies, take a strip of muslin, one inch wide and long enough to go around the pie and lap, wet the cloth in cold water and lay it around like a binding, half upon the pie and half upon the plate, pressing it either side, when the pie is baked remove cloth. Another way:—Make a small opening in the upper crust and insert a little roll of brown paper perpendicularly. The steam will escape as from a chimney, all the juice will be retained. Another:—Cut a narrow strip of crust for the edge of pie, dip it in water and put it between two crusts pressing the upper one down. This forms a paste which joins the crusts and prevents the juice from escaping. All juicy pies should be baked as soon as they are filled and in a quick oven.

To make steak tender, lay it on a flat dish in a mixture of three tablespoons salad oil and one of vinegar and let it remain half hour on each side, then fry.

Raisins may be seeded quickly by scalding them.

Never allow fresh meats to remain in paper, it absorbs the juice.

Salt will curdle new milk; in making custards, gravies, etc. the salt should not be added until the dish is prepared.

Salt is good for cleaning marble, wash basins, sink fixtures and the like.

Glassware that have had milk in them should never be put in hot water.

Too much salt in bread will stop fermentation.

A small cup of mashed potatoes are nice in corncakes when eggs are scarce.

Milk for custard pies should always be scalded and cooled, before putting in the crust.

A small piece of ginger root in the lard will prevent doughnuts from soaking fat.

Always put a pinch of soda in milk that is to be boiled, as an acid is formed by boiling.

A little sulphate potassa added to preserves prevents fermentation.

A piece of charcoal put in pot of boiling cabbage will do away with the strong odor.

When you boil cabbage tie a bit of dry bread in a bag and put it in the kettle. You will not be troubled with the usual disagreeable odor.

When beaten eggs are to be mixed with hot milk as in making custards or gravies, dip the hot milk into the beaten eggs a spoonful at a time, stirring well each time until the eggs are well thinned, then add both together.

A solution of washing soda is excellent for solid plated or nickel-ware for cleaning. Rub thoroughly dry.

Colgate's Dermal Skin Soap is excellent for keeping the hands soft and smooth.

Cure For Diphtheria.

Put one teaspoon of flour of sulphur into a wine glass of water and stir with the finger instead of a spoon. When well mixed give it as a gargle.

For Burns and Scalds

Pure vaseline is excellent; also, lime water and linseed oil, equal portions; either one should be kept in a convenient place.

INDEX.

THE ONLY

PURE, CLEAN, HEALTHFUL

BAKING POWDER

MADE.

NO AMMONIA.   NO ALUM.

EVERY

CAN

GUARAN-

TEED.

SNOW FLAKE

TWELVE   OUNCES

TRADE MARK

BAKING POWDER

USED EXCLUSIVELY BY THE U. S. GOVERNMENT.

HEADQUARTERS DEPARTMENT OF DAKOTA,
Office Chief Commissary of Subsistance,
ST. PAUL, MINN., Dec. 28, 1891.

MR. C. R. GROFF, St. Paul, Minn.:

SIR:—I enclose one copy of the contract made with you for SNOW FLAKE Baking Powder.   Respectfully,

Your obedient servant,

THOS. C. SULLIVAN,
Lieut. Col. and A. C. G. S., Chief C. S.

www.ingramcontent.com/pod-product-compliance
Lightning Source LLC
Chambersburg PA
CBHW031442280326
41927CB00038B/1506